BIRDS IN LONDON

BIRDS IN LONDON

By

W. H. HUDSON

A Reprint with an Introduction by
Richard Fitter

DAVID & CHARLES REPRINTS

7153 4690 3

Birds in London was first published by
Longmans Green & Co in 1898
This edition published in 1969

Printed in Great Britain by
Clarke Doble & Brendon Limited Plymouth
for David & Charles (Publishers) Limited
South Devon House Newton Abbot
Devon

FOREWORD TO THE 1969 EDITION

W. H. HUDSON—nobody would ever think of referring to him, in the modern fashion, as William Hudson, and the idea of calling him Bill positively makes one swoon —is one of the few writers of any literary quality to have written about British birds. Londoners should count themselves fortunate that circumstances, which he did not specify, obliged Hudson to spend the summers of 1896 and 1897 'in town'. From this enforced exile grew one of his most attractive books, still not only almost compulsively readable but a quarry of facts on a subject which, as he himself complained, had hitherto been only imperfectly investigated. Since Hudson wrote *Birds in London* there have been other books on the avifauna of the metropolis—I have written one myself —but it is safe to say that, unlike Hudson's, none will live anywhere but in the bibliographies of specialists. *Birds in London* has been reprinted more than once in various editions, and was in regular demand until the 1930s, when much of its factual information was long out of date. I am therefore particularly glad to have been given the opportunity to introduce a further edition which, it is to be hoped, will keep the book's memory green till it celebrates its centenary in 1998.

The London and Londoners of today are more different from those of Hudson's day than the sage himself would have conceived possible, and inevitably the birds too have changed. No longer is Hampstead Heath on the edge of open country. No longer do birdcatchers attempt to ply their illegal trade in the London parks. And can one imagine the columns of *The Times* today, after the authorities responsible for the upkeep of Kensington Gardens had ordered the trees of a rookery to be felled? In Hudson's day the gulls had only just started to come up the Thames from the estuary, and the first welcome they received was a volley of shots from the bridges. Today one of the features of the London winter scene is the sight of clouds of screaming gulls clustered around the upper windows of tall office blocks, as the secretaries, and I daresay some-times the managing director too, throw them the remains of their lunches, T. D. Pigott, one of Hudson's con-temporaries as a writer on London birds, once saw a London cabby strike sharply with his whip at a yellow-hammer that was feeding in the gutter by his cab-stand. Such an incident is almost impossible to imagine in modern London, even translated into a taxi-man hurling a spanner at a pigeon on the pavement. On the other hand, Hudson describes how men would spend their Sundays wandering over Hackney Marshes, aimlessly shooting at starlings, larks and pigeons, and it must be admitted that in many remoter suburban areas, though not in as public a place as Hackney Marshes, the same aimless shooting by gangs of youths can still be seen.

The crow tribe were Hudson's greatest favourites among the birds of London. He knew the carrion crow, rook and jackdaw. Today he would still find the crow lording it over the inner parks, and still kept under some control in the interests of the water fowl, whose eggs they steal. The rook has long gone, its last rookery, in Gray's Inn, having been deserted during the First World War, and a rook is now one of the most unusual London birds. The jackdaw is still, as it was in Hudson's day, a London rarity, the last small colony hanging grimly on in the south-western corner of Kensington Gardens. But to balance the loss of the rook the jay has returned, and it may not be long before the magpie, which has adapted itself to town life elsewhere in Europe, returns too. When Hudson wrote, the London park woodpigeons were a great novelty; now the woodpigeon is one of the universal London birds, nesting almost wherever there is a tree or two. The stock dove, as in Hudson's time, is still somewhat of a rarity that comes and goes. Starlings were only just beginning to roost in Central London in the late '90s, and the transition to buildings from the original roosts in trees on the islands in the park lakes was still some years ahead. Today the nightly gatherings of starlings on buildings in Trafalgar Square and many other parts of the centre of London is one of the sights of the town all through the autumn and winter.

Great changes have come about too in the water birds of London. The gulls have left the river and invaded the parks, patrolling also over the whole built-up area in search of food during the winter months. The dabchick, which had just colonised the park lakes in the '90s, has now gone, but is replaced by innumerable moorhens and coots. Mallards were certainly in the parks when Hudson roamed them, as he describes in a typical incident on pp 38–9:

It is a curious and delightful experience to be alone on a damp autumn night in Kensington Gardens. One is surrounded by London; its dull continuous murmur may be heard, and the glinting of distant lamps catches the eye through the trees; these fitful gleams and distant sounds but make the silence and darkness all the more deep and impressive. Suddenly the whistling of wings is heard, and the loud startled cry of the mallard, as the birds, vaguely seen, rush by overhead; the effect on the mind is wonderful—one has been transported as by a miracle into the midst of a wild and solitary nature.

Whether tufted ducks and pochards, both so common today, were among the many mallard that scrambled for the food which the park authorities provided on the Serpentine, Hudson does not say. Indeed one sometimes wonders if he would have been capable of identifying them. He certainly once committed himself to the statement, astonishing to a modern bird watcher, that in winter plumage it is almost impossible to distinguish the black-headed from the common gull.

This brings out one of the great changes that have occurred in bird watching since the end of the last century, the enormous increase in the skill of bird watchers in identifying birds in the field. Serious bird watchers of that time were almost obliged to shoot any strange bird in order to identify it. Nobody believed a purely sight record, because it was thought that most birds, and certainly rare ones, could not be identified with any confidence except in the hand. How Hudson would have been astonished—and gratified —at the great numbers of people today who, sometimes with their identification guide in hand, will confidently polish off the five common gulls as the first lesson in the beginner's course, and later graduate to attempting to separate the chiffchaff from the willow warbler without even hearing their voice. It is, of course, a very good thing that this change has taken place. What matters it if some birds are sometimes wrongly identified, compared with the wounding of the human spirit involved in shooting a bird merely to satisfy an idle, or even a scientific, curiosity?

In Hudson's day serious naturalists were either egg

and skin collectors, if they studied birds; butterfly or beetle collectors, if they were 'bug hunters', as the phrase then went; or owners of private herbaria, if their bent lay towards botany. Today, except in entomology, the private collector is almost extinct, and fashion has mercifully swung towards observation, photography and conservation. The modern naturalist is catered for by a bewildering medley of voluntary bodies, which roughly speaking resolve themselves into the natural history societies, whose umbrella body is the Natural History Societies Committee of the Council for Nature, and the county naturalists' trusts, which are all represented on the County Naturalists' Trusts Committee of the Society for the Promotion of Nature Reserves. The observers and photographers belong to the natural history societies, and the conservationists and country-lovers join the county trusts. Often, of course, the two are the same, and many naturalists belong to both a society and a trust. For the London area the London Natural History Society covers the whole region within twenty miles of St Paul's Cathedral, and there are also county societies or field clubs for Hertfordshire, Essex and Kent, as well as many more local bodies. Likewise there are naturalists' trusts covering Essex, Kent, Surrey, and Hertfordshire and Middlesex combined, as well as all the other counties in England and Wales; Buckinghamshire goes in with Berkshire and Oxfordshire. As addresses of all these bodies, both central and local, are liable to change, I do not print them here, but shall be happy to supply them, for any district in Great Britain, to any reader who sends me a stamped addressed postcard c/o the publishers.

RICHARD FITTER

BIRDS IN LONDON

'THE CROW WITH HIS VOICE OF CARE'

BIRDS IN LONDON

BY

W. H. HUDSON, F.Z.S.

ILLUSTRATED BY BRYAN HOOK, A. D. McCORMICK
AND FROM PHOTOGRAPHS FROM NATURE BY R. B. LODGE

LONGMANS, GREEN, AND CO.
39 PATERNOSTER ROW, LONDON
NEW YORK AND BOMBAY
1898

PREFACE

THE opening chapter contains, by way of introduction, all that need be said concerning the
object and scope of this work; it remains to
say here that, as my aim has been to furnish an
account of the London wild bird life of to-day,
there was little help to be had from the writings
of previous observers. These mostly deal with
the central parks, and are interesting now,
mainly, as showing the changes that have taken
place. At the end of the volume a list will be
found of the papers and books on the subject
which are known to me. This list will strike
many readers as an exceedingly meagre one,
when it is remembered that London has always
been a home of ornithologists—that from the
days of Oliver Goldsmith, who wrote pleasantly

of the Temple Gardens rookery, and of Thomas
Pennant and his friend Daines Barrington, there
have never been wanting observers of the wild
bird life within our gates. The fact remains
that, with the exception of a few incidental
passages to be found in various ornithological
works, nothing was expressly written about
the birds of London until James Jennings's
' Ornithologia ' saw the light a little over seventy
years ago. Jennings's work was a poem,
probably the worst ever written in the English
language ; but as he inserted copious notes,
fortunately in prose, embodying his own observations on the bird life of east and south-east
London, the book has a very considerable
interest for us to-day. Nothing more of importance appeared until the late Shirley Hibberd's
lively paper on ' London Birds ' in 1865. From
that date onward the subject has attracted an
increased attention, and at present we have a
number of London or park naturalists, as they
might be called, who view the resident London
species as adapted to an urban life, and who
chronicle their observations in the ' Field,'

' Nature,' ' Zoologist,' ' Nature Notes,' and other natural history journals, and in the newspapers and magazines.

To return to the present work. Treating of actualities I have been obliged for the most part to gather my own materials, relying perhaps too much on my own observation; since London is now too vast a field for any person, however diligent, to know it intimately in all its extent.

Probably any reader who is an observer of birds on his own account, and has resided for some years near a park or other open space in London, will be able to say, by way of criticism, that I have omitted some important or interesting fact known to him—something that ought to have had a place in a work of this kind. In such a case I can only plead either that the fact was not known to me, or that I had some good reason for not using it. Moreover, there is a limit to the amount of matter which can be included in a book of this kind, and a selection had to be made from a large number of facts and anecdotes I had got together.

All the matter contained in this book, with the exception of one article, or part of an article, on London birds, in the 'Saturday Review,' now appears for the first time.

In conclusion, I have to express my warm thanks to those who have helped me in my task, by supplying me with fresh information, and in other ways.

W. H. H.

London : *April*, 1898.

CONTENTS

CHAPTER IV

THE LONDON DAW

CHAPTER V

EXPULSION OF THE ROOKS

CHAPTER VI

RECENT COLONISTS

CHAPTER VII

LONDON'S LITTLE BIRDS

CHAPTER VIII

MOVEMENTS OF LONDON BIRDS

CHAPTER IX

A SURVEY OF THE PARKS : WEST LONDON

CHAPTER XIII

SOUTH-WEST LONDON

CHAPTER XIV

PROTECTION OF BIRDS IN THE PARKS

LIST OF ILLUSTRATIONS

PLATES

ILLUSTRATIONS IN TEXT

BIRDS IN LONDON

---◆◇◆---

CHAPTER I

THE BIRDS AND THE BOOK

A handbook of London birds considered—Reasons for not
writing it—Changes in the character of the wild bird
population, and supposed cause—The London sparrow—Its
abundance — Bread-begging habits — Monotony — Its best
appearance—Beautiful finches—Value of open spaces—The
sparrows' afternoon tea in Hyde Park—Purpose of this book.

AMONG the many little schemes and more or
less good intentions which have flitted about my
brain like summer flies in a room, there was one
for a small volume on London birds ; to contain,
for principal matter, lists of the species resident
throughout the year, of the visitants, regular
and occasional, and of the vanished species
which have inhabited the metropolis in recent,
former, or historical times.   For everyone, even
the veriest Dryasdust among us, has some glow
of poetic feeling in him, some lingering regret

for the beautiful that has vanished and returneth
not ; consequently, it would be hard in treating
of London bird life not to go back to times
which now seem very ancient, when the kite
was common—the city's soaring scavenger,
protected by law, just as the infinitely less
attractive turkey-buzzard is now protected in
some towns of the western world. Again,
thanks to Mr. Harting's researches into old
records, we have the account of beautiful white
spoonbills, associated with herons, building their
nests on the tree-tops in the Bishop of London's
grounds at Fulham.

To leave this fascinating theme. It struck
me at first that the book vaguely contemplated
might be made useful to lovers and students of
bird life in London ; and I was also encouraged
by the thought that the considerable amount of
printed material which exists relating to the
subject would make the task of writing it comparatively easy.

But I no sooner looked attentively into the
subject than I saw how difficult it really was,
and how unsatisfactory, and I might almost add
useless, the work would prove.

To begin with, what is London ? It is a

very big town, a 'province covered with houses';
but for the ornithologist where, on any side,
does the province end ?   Does it end five miles
south of Charing Cross, at Sydenham, or ten miles
further afield, at Downe ?   Or, looking north, do
we draw the line at Hampstead, or Aldenham ?
The whole metropolitan area has, let us say, a
circumference of about ninety miles, and within
its outermost irregular boundary there is room
for half a dozen concentric lines, each of which
will contain a London, differing greatly in size
and, in a much less degree, in character.   If the
list be made to include all the birds found in
such rural and even wild places—woods, thickets,
heaths, and marshes—as exist within a sixteen-
mile radius, it is clear that most of the inland
species found in the counties of Kent, Surrey,
Middlesex, Hertfordshire, and Essex would be
in it.

The fact is, in drawing up a list of London
birds, the writer can, within limits, make it as
long or short as he thinks proper.   Thus, if he
wishes to have a long list, and is partial to
round numbers, he will be able to get a century
of species by making his own twelve or thirteen
mile radius.   Should he then alter his mind,

and think that a modest fifty would content him,
all he would have to do to get that number
would be to contract his line, bringing it somewhere near the indeterminate borders of inner
London, where town and country mix or pass
into each other.   Now a handbook written on
this plan would be useful only if a very exact
boundary were drawn, and the precise locality
given in which each resident or breeding species
had its haunts, where the student or lover of
birds could watch or listen for it with some
chance of being rewarded.   Even so, the book
would not serve its purpose for a longer period
than two or three years; after three years it
would most certainly be out of date, so great and
continuous is the growth of London on all sides.
Thus, going round London, keeping to that
partly green indeterminate borderland already
mentioned, there are many little hidden rustic
spots where in the summer of 1897 the woodpecker, green and spotted, and the nuthatch and
tree-creeper bred; also the nightingale, bottle-
tit, and wryneck, and jay and crow, and kestrel
and white and brown owl; but who can say
that they will breed in the same places in 1899,
or even in 1898 ?   For these little green rustic

refuges are situated on the lower slopes of a volcano, which is always in a state of eruption, and year by year they are being burnt up and obliterated by ashes and lava.

After I had at once and for ever dropped, for the reasons stated, all idea of a handbook, the thought remained that there was still much to be said about London bird life which might be useful, although in another way. The subject was often in my mind during the summer months of 1896 and 1897, which, for my sins, I was compelled to spend in town. During this wasted and dreary period, when I was often in the parks and open spaces in all parts of London, I was impressed more than I had been before with the changes constantly going on in the character of the bird population of the metropolis. These changes are not rapid enough to show a marked difference in a space of two or three years; but when we take a period of fifteen or twenty years, they strike us as really very great. They are the result of the gradual decrease in numbers and final dying out of many of the old-established species, chiefly singing birds, and, at the same time, the appearance of other species previously unknown in London, and their increase and diffusion. Considering these two facts, one is inclined to say off-hand that the diminution or dying out of one set of species is simply due to the fact that they are incapable of thriving in the conditions in which they are placed; that the London smoke is fatal in the long run to some of the more delicate birds, as it undoubtedly is to the rose and other plants that require pure air and plenty of sunshine; and that, on the other hand, the new colonists that are increasing are species of a coarser fibre, greater vitality, and able, like the plane-tree in the plant world, to thrive in such conditions. It is really not so: the tits and finches, the robin, wren, hedge-sparrow, pied wagtail, some of the warblers, and the missel-thrush, are as vigorous and well able to live in London as the wood-pigeon. They are, moreover, very much more prolific than the pigeon, and find their food with greater ease. Yet we see that these lively, active species are dying out, while the slow, heavy dove, which must eat largely to live, and lays but two eggs on a frail platform of sticks for nest, is rapidly increasing.

Here then, it seemed, was a subject which it might be for the advantage of the bird-lovers in London to consider; and I write in the conviction that there are as many Londoners who love the sight and sound of wild bird life as there are who find refreshment in trees and grass and flowers, who are made glad by the sight of a blue sky, to whom the sunshine is sweet and pleasant to behold.

In going about London, after my mind had begun to dwell on this subject, I was frequently amused, and sometimes teased, by the sight and sound of the everywhere-present multitudinous sparrow. In London there are no grain-growers and market-gardeners, consequently there is no tiresome sparrow question, and no sparrow-clubs to vex the tender-hearted. These sparrows were not to be thought about in their relation to agriculture, but were simply little birds, too often, in many a weary mile, in many an unlovely district, the only representatives of the avian class, flying to and fro, chirping and chirruping from dawn to dark; nor birds only: I had them also for butterflies, seen sometimes in crowds and clouds, as in the tropics, with no rich nor splendid colouring on their wings ; and I had them for cicadas, and noisy locusts of arboreal habits, hundreds and thousands of them, whirring in a subdued way in the park trees during the sultry hours. They were all these things and scavengers as well, ever busy at their scavengering in the dusty and noisy ways ; everywhere finding some organic matter to comfort their little stomachs, or to carry to their nestlings.

At times the fanciful idea would occur to me that I was on a commission appointed to inquire into the state of the wild bird life of London, or some such subject, and that my fellow commissioners were sparrows, so incessantly were they with me, though in greatly varying numbers, during my perambulations.

After all, the notion that they attended or accompanied me in my walks was not wholly fanciful. For no sooner does any person enter any public garden or park, or other open space where there are trees, than, if he be not too absorbed in his own thoughts, he will see that several sparrows are keeping him company, flying from tree to tree, or bush to bush, alighting occasionally on the ground near him, watching

his every movement ; and if he sit down on a
chair or bench several of them will come close
to him, and hop this way and that before him,
uttering a little plaintive note of interrogation—
Have you got nothing for us? They have come
to look on every human being who walks among
the park trees and round the garden-beds as a
mere perambulating machine for the distribution
of fragments of bread. The sparrow's theory or
philosophy of life, from our point of view, is
very ridiculous, but he finds it profitable, and
wants no better.

I remember that during those days, when
the little creatures were so much with me,
whether I wanted them or no, some person
wrote to one of the newspapers to say that he
had just made the acquaintance of the common
sparrow in a new character. The sparrow was
and always had been a familiar bird to him, but
he had never previously seen it gathered in
crowds at its ' afternoon tea ' in Hyde Park, a
spectacle which he had now witnessed with
surprise and pleasure.

If (I thought) this innumerous feathered
company could only be varied somewhat, the
modest plumage retouched, by Nature, with

harmonious olive green and yellow tints, pure greys and pure browns, with rose, carmine, tile and chestnut reds ; and if the monotonous little burly forms could be reshaped, and made in some cases larger, in others smaller, some burlier still and others slimmer, more delicate and aërial in appearance, the spectacle of their afternoon tea would be infinitely more attractive and refreshing than it now is to many a Londoner's tired eyes.

Their voices, too—for the refashioned mixed crowd would have a various language, like the species that warble and twitter and call musically to one another in orchard and copse— would give a new and strange delight to the listener.

No doubt the sparrow is, to quote the letter-writer's expression, ' a jolly little fellow,' quite friendly with his supposed enemy man, amusing in his tea-table manners, and deserving of all the praise and crumbs we give him. He is even more. To those who have watched him begging for and deftly catching small scraps of bread, suspended like a hawk-moth in the air before the giving hand, displaying his conspicuous black gorget and the pale ash colour of his under

surface, while his rapidly vibrating wings are
made silky and translucent by the sunlight

PARK SPARROW
BEGGING

passing through
them, he appears,
indeed, a pretty
and even graceful
creature.

But he is, after all, only a
common sparrow, a mean representative of bird life in our midst ; in
all the æsthetic qualities which make
birds charming—beauty of form and
colour, grace of motion, and melody
—less than the least of the others.
Therefore to greatly praise him is to publish

our ignorance, or, at all events, to make it appear that he is admired because, being numerous and familiar with man, he has been closely and well looked at, while the wilder and less common species have only been seen at a distance, and therefore indistinctly.

A distinguished American writer on birds once visited England in order to make the acquaintance of our most noted feathered people, and in his haste pronounced the chaffinch the ' prettiest British songster.' Doubtless he had seen it oftenest, and closely, and at its best ; but he would never have expressed such an opinion if he had properly seen many other British singing birds ; if, for instance (confining our-selves to the fringilline family), he had seen his ' shilfa's ' nearest relation, the brambling, in his black dress beautifully variegated with buff and brown ; or the many-coloured cirl-bunting ; or that golden image of a bird, the yellow-hammer ; or the green siskin, ' that lovely little oddity,' seeking his food, tit-like, among the pine needles, or clinging to pendulous twigs ; or the linnet in his spring plumage—pale grey and richest brown and carmine—singing among the flowery gorse ; or the goldfinch, flitting amidst the apple-bloom in May, or feeding on the thistle in July and August, clinging to the downy heads, twittering as he passes from plant to plant, showing his gay livery of crimson, black, and gold ; or the sedentary bullfinch, a miniature hawk in appearance, with a wonderful rose-coloured breast, sitting among the clustering leaves of a dark evergreen—yew or holly.

Beautiful birds are all these, and there are others just as beautiful in other passerine families, but alas ! they are at a distance from us ; they live in the country, and it is only that small ' whiff of the country ' to be enjoyed in a public park which fate allows to the majority of Londoners, the many thousands of toilers from year's end to year's end, and their wives and children.

To those of us who take an annual holiday, and, in addition, an occasional run in the country, or who are not bound to town, it is hardly possible to imagine how much is meant by that little daily or weekly visit to a park. Its value to the confined millions has accordingly never been, and probably cannot be, rightly estimated. For the poor who have not those

periods of refreshment which others consider so
necessary to their health and contentment, the
change from the close, adulterated atmosphere
of the workshop and the living-room, and stone-
paved noisy street, to the open, green, comparatively quiet park, is indeed great, and its benefit
to body and mind incalculable. The sight of
the sun; of the sky, no longer a narrow strip,
but wide, infinite over all; the freshness of the
unconfined air which the lungs drink in; the
green expanse of earth, and large trees standing
apart, away from houses—all this produces a
shock of strange pleasure and quickens the tired
pulse with sudden access of life. In a small
way—sad it is to think in how small a way!—
it is a return to nature, an escape for the
moment from the prison and sick-room of un-
natural conditions; and the larger and less
artificial the park or open space, and the more
abounding in wild, especially bird, life, the more
restorative is the effect.

It is indeed invariably the animal life which
exercises the greatest attraction and is most
exhilarating. It is really pathetic to see how
many persons of the working class come every
day, all the year round, but especially in the

summer months, to that minute transcript of
wild nature in Hyde Park at the spot called the
Dell, where the Serpentine ends.   They are
drawn thither by the birds—the multitude of
sparrows that gather to be fed, and the wood-
pigeons, and a few moorhens that live in the
rushes.

' I call these my chickens, and I'm obliged
to come every day to feed them,' said a paralytic-
looking white-haired old man in the shabbiest
clothes, one evening as I stood there; then,
taking some fragments of stale bread from his
pockets, he began feeding the sparrows, and
while doing so he chuckled with delight, and
looked round from time to time to see if the
others were enjoying the spectacle.

To   him   succeeded   two   sedate-looking
labourers, big, strong men, with tired, dusty
faces, on their way home from work.   Each
produced from his coat-pocket a little store of
fragments of bread and meat, saved from the
midday meal, carefully wrapped up in a piece
of newspaper.   After bestowing their scraps on
the   little   brown-coated   crowd,   one   spoke :
' Come on, mate, they've had it all, and now let's
go home and see what the missus has got for

our tea'; and home they trudged across the park, with hearts refreshed and lightened, no doubt, to be succeeded by others and still others, London workmen and their wives and children, until the sun had set and the birds were all gone.

Here then is an object lesson which no person who is capable of reading the emotions in the countenance, who has any sympathy with his fellow-creatures, can fail to be impressed by. Not only at that spot in Hyde Park may it be seen, but at all the parks and open spaces in London; in some more than others, as at St. James's Park, where the gulls are fed during the winter months, and at Battersea and Regent's Parks, where the starlings congregate every evening in July and August. What we see is the perpetual hunger of the heart and craving of those who are compelled to live apart from Nature, who have only these momentary glimpses of her face, and of the refreshment they experience at sight of trees and grass and water, and, above everything, of wild and glad animal life. How important, then, that the most should be made of our few suitable open spaces; that everything possible should be done to maintain

in them an abundant and varied wild bird life!
Unfortunately, this has not been seen, else we
should not have lost so much, especially in the
royal parks. In some of the parks under the
County Council there are great signs of improvement, an evident anxiety to protect and
increase the stock of wild birds; but even here
the most zealous of the superintendents are not
fully conscious of the value of what they are
themselves doing. They are encouraging the
wild birds because they are considered 'ornaments' to the park, just as they plant rhodo-
dendrons and other exotic shrubs that have big
gaily-coloured flowers in their season, and as
they exhibit some foreign bird of gorgeous
plumage in the park aviary. They have not
yet grasped the fact—I hope Mr. Sexby, the
excellent head of the parks department, will
pardon my saying it—that the feathered inhabitants of our open spaces are something more
than 'ornaments'; that the sight and sound of
any wild bird, from the croaking carrion crow
to the small lyrical kitty wren or tinkling tom-
tit, will afford more pleasure to the Londoner—
in other words, conduce more to his health and

happiness—than all the gold pheasants and other brightly-apparelled prisoners, native and foreign, to be seen in the park cages.

From the foregoing it will be seen that this little book, which comes in place of the one I had, in a vague way, once thought of writing, is in some degree a book with a purpose. Birds are not considered merely as objects of interest to the ornithologist and to a few other persons—objects or creatures which the great mass of the people of the metropolis have really nothing to do with, and vaguely regard as something at a distance, of no practical import, or as wholly unrelated to their urban life. Rather they are considered as a necessary part of those pleasure- and health-giving transcripts of nature which we retain and cherish as our best possessions—the open sun-lit and tree-shaded spaces, green with grass and bright with water; so important a part indeed, as bringing home to us that glad freedom and wildness which is our best medicine, that without it all the rest would lose much of its virtue.

But on this point—the extreme pleasure

which the confined Londoner experiences in seeing and hearing wild birds, and the consequent value of our wild bird life—enough has been said in this place, as it will be necessary to return to the subject in one of the concluding chapters.

CHAPTER II

THERE are not many crows in London; the
number of the birds that are left are indeed few,
and, if we exclude the magpie and jay, there are
only three species. But the magpie and jay
cannot be left out altogether, when we find both
species still existing at a distance of six and a
half to seven miles from Charing Cross. The
magpie is all but lost; at the present time there
are no more than four birds inhabiting inner
London, doubtless escaped from captivity, and
afraid to leave the parks in which they found
refuge—those islands of verdure in the midst of
a sea, or desert, of houses. One bird, the sur-
vivor of a pair, has his home in St. James's Park,
and is the most interesting figure in that haunt

of birds; a spirited creature, a great hater and persecutor of the carrion crows when they come. The other three consort together in Regent's Park; once or twice they have built a nest, but

THE LAST RAVEN

failed to hatch their eggs. Probably all three are females. When, some time ago, the 'Son of the Marshes' wrote that the magpie had been extirpated in his own county of Surrey, and that to see it he should have to visit the London parks, he made too much of these escaped birds, which may be numbered on the fingers of one hand. Yet we know that the pie was formerly—even in this

century—quite common in London. Yarrell, in
his 'British Birds,' relates that he once saw
twenty-three together in Kensington Gardens.
In these gardens they bred, probably for the last
time, in 1856. Nor, so far as I know, do any
magpies survive in the woods and thickets on
the outskirts of the metropolis, except at two
spots in the south-west district. The fate of
the last pair at Hampstead has been related
by Harting, in Lobley's 'Hampstead Hill'
(London, 1889). For several years this pair had
their nest in an unclimbable tree at the Grove;
at length, one of the pair was shot by a local
bird-stuffer, after which the surviving bird twice
found and returned with a new mate; but one
by one all were killed by the same miscreant.

It would be easy enough for any person to
purchase a few magpies in the market and
liberate them in St. James's and Regent's Parks,
and other suitable places, where, if undisturbed,
they would certainly breed; but I fear that it
would not be an advisable thing to do at present,
on account of the very strong prejudice which
exists against this handsome bird. Thus, at St.
James's Park the one surviving bird is ' one too
many.' according to the keepers. 'One for

sorrow ' is an old saying. He is, they say, a robber and a teaser, dangerous to the ornamental water-fowl in the breeding season, a great persecutor of the wood-pigeons, and in summer never happy unless he has a pigeon's egg in his beak. It strikes one forcibly that this is not a faithful portrait—that the magpie has been painted all black, instead of black and white as nature made him. At all events, we know that during the first two or three decades of the present century there was an abundant and varied wild bird life in the royal parks, and that at the same time the magpies were more numerous there than they are now known to be in any forest or wild place in England.

The jay does not inhabit any of the inner parks and open spaces ; nor is there any evidence of its having been a resident London species at any time. But it is found in the most rural parts and in the wooded outskirts of the metropolis. Its haunts will be mentioned in the chapters descriptive of the parks and open spaces.

There is no strong prejudice against the jay among the park keepers, and I am glad to know that, in two or three parks, attempts will be made shortly to introduce this most beautiful

of British birds.   It is to be hoped that when we
have got him his occasional small peccadilloes
will not be made too much of.

The raven has long been lost to London, but
not so long as might be imagined when we
consider how nearly extinct this noble species,
as an inland breeder, now is in all the southern
half, and very nearly all the northern half, of
England.   It is not my intention in this book to
go much into the past history of London bird
life, but I make an exception of the raven on
account of an extreme partiality for that most
human-like of feathered creatures.   Down to
about the middle of last century, perhaps later,
the raven was a common London bird.   He
was, after the kite had vanished, the principal
feathered scavenger, and it was said that a
London raven could easily be distinguished from
a country bird by his dulled or dusty-looking
plumage, the result of his food-seeking opera-
tions in dust and ash heaps.   A little way out
of the metropolis he lingered on, as a breeding
species, down to within a little more than half
a century ago ; the last pair, so far as I can
discover, bred at Enfield down to about 1845.

The original ' raven tree ' on which this pair had nested for many years was cut down, after which the birds built a nest in a clump of seven elm-trees, known locally as the ' seven sisters,' five of which are still standing.

In London the last pair had ceased to breed about twenty years earlier ; and of a hundred histories of ' last ravens ' to be met with in all parts of the country, that of these London birds is by no means the least interesting, and is worth relating again.

Down to about 1826 this pair bred annually on one of the large elms in Hyde Park, until it entered into the head of one of the park keepers to pull down the nest containing young birds. The name and subsequent history of this injurious wretch have not been handed down. Doubtless he has long gone to his account ; and let us add the pious wish that his soul, along with the souls of all those who were wanton destroyers of man's feathered fellow-creatures, is now being driven, like a snow-flake, round and round the icy pole in that everlasting whirlwind described by Courthope in his ' Paradise of Birds.'

The old ravens, deprived of their young, forsook the park. One of the young birds was successfully reared by the keeper ; and the story of this raven was long afterwards related by Jesse. He was allowed the fullest liberty, and as he passed a good deal of his time in the vicinity of the Row, he came to be very well known to all those who were accustomed to walk in Hyde Park at that time. He was fond of the society of the men then engaged in the construction of Rennie's bridge over the Serpentine, and the workmen made a pet of him. His favourite amusement was to sidle cunningly up to some passer-by or idler, and, watching his chance, give him or her a sharp dig on the ankle with his beak. One day a fashionably dressed lady was walking near the bridge, when all at once catching sight of the bird at her feet, on feeling its sharp beak prodding her heel, she screamed and gave a great start, and in starting dropped a valuable gold bracelet from her wrist. No sooner did the jewel touch the ground than the raven snatched it up in his beak and flew away with it into Kensington Gardens, where it was searched for, but never found. It was believed that he made use of one of the hollow trees in the gardens as a hiding place for plunder of this kind. At length

the raven disappeared—some one had stolen
him ; but after an absence of several weeks he
reappeared in the park with clipped wings. His
disposition, too, had suffered a change : he moped
a good deal, and finally one morning was found
dead in the Serpentine. It was surmised that
he had drowned himself from grief at having
been deprived of the power of flight.

A few ravens have since visited London. In
1850 a keeper in Regent's Park observed two of
these birds engaged in a savage fight, which
ended in the death of one of the combatants.

In March 1890 a solitary raven appeared in
Kensington Gardens, and remained there for
several weeks. A keeper informed me that it
was captured and taken away. If this unfortunate raven had known his London better, he
would not have chosen a royal park for a
residence.

Was this Kensington raven, it has been
asked, a wild bird, or a strayed pet, or an escaped
captive ? I believe the following incident will
throw some light on the question.

For many years past two or three ravens have
usually been kept at the Tower of London.
About seven years ago, as near as I can make

out, there were two birds, male and female, and they paired and set to work building a nest on a tree. By and by, for some unknown reason, they demolished the nest they had made and started building a new one in another place. This nest also failed to satisfy them and was pulled to pieces like the first, and another begun; and finally, after half a dozen such attempts, the cock bird, who was a strong flyer, abandoned the task altogether and took to roaming about London, possibly in search of a new mate with a better knowledge of nest-building. It was his habit to mount up to a considerable height in the air, and soar about above the Tower, then to fly away to St. Paul's Cathedral, where he would perch on the cross above the dome and survey the raree-show beneath. Then he would wing his way to the docks, or in some other direction; and day by day his wanderings over London were extended, until the owner or owners of the bird were warned that if his wings were not clipped he would, soon or late, be lost.

But when it was at last resolved to cut his wings he refused to be caught. He had grown shy and suspicious, and although he came for food and to roost on one of the turrets every evening, he would not allow any person to come too near him. After some weeks of this semi-independent life he finally disappeared, having, as I believe, met his end in Kensington Gardens.

His old mate 'Jenny,' as she is named, still lives at the Tower. I hear she has just been provided with a new mate.

Three other crows remain—the carrion crow, rook, and jackdaw, all black but comely, although not beautiful nor elegant, like the bright vari-coloured jay and the black and white pie. Unfortunately they are a small remnant, and we are threatened with the near loss of one, if not of all. The first-named of this corvine trio is now the largest and most important wild bird that has been left to us; if any as big or bigger appear, they are but casual visitors—a chance cormorant in severe weather, and the heron, that sometimes comes by night to the ornamental waters in the parks in search of fish, to vanish again, grey and ghostlike in the grey dawn.

It is curious to find that the big, loud-voiced, hated carrion crow—so conspicuous and aggressive a bird—has a firmer hold on life in the metropolis than his two relations, the rook and daw; for these two are sociable in habits and inclined to be domestic, and are everywhere inhabitants of towns. Or, rather, it would be strange but for the fact that the crow is less generally disliked in London than out of it.

Now, although these our three surviving crows are being left far behind in actual numbers by some other species that have only recently established themselves among us, and are moreover decreasing, and may be wholly lost at no distant date, they have been so long connected with London, and historically, as well as on account of their high intelligence and interesting habits, are so much more to us than the birds of other families, that I am tempted to write at considerable length about them, devoting a separate chapter to each species. I also cherish the hope that their threatened loss may yet be prevented ; doubtless every Londoner. will agree that it would be indeed a pity to lose these old residents.

It is a fact, although perhaps not a quite familiar one, that those who reside in the metropolis are more interested in and have a kindlier

feeling for their wild birds than is the case in
the rural districts. The reason is not far to
seek : the poorer we are the more do we prize
our small belongings. A wind-fluttered green
leaf, a sweet-smelling red rose, a thrush in song,
is naturally more to a Londoner than to the
dweller in mid-Surrey, or Kent, or Devon.

CHAPTER III

THE CARRION CROW IN THE BALANCE

The crow in London—Persecuted in the royal parks—Degrada-
tion of Hyde Park—Ducks in the Serpentine: how they are
thinned—Shooting a chicken with a revolver—Habits of the
Hyde Park mallard—Anecdotes—Number of London crows
—The crow a long-lived bird; a bread-eater—Anecdote—
Seeks its food on the river—The crow as a pet—Anecdotes.

THE carrion crow has probably always been an
inhabitant of the central parks ; at all events it
is well known that for a long time past a pair
bred annually in the trees on the north side of
the Serpentine, down to within the last three
years.　As these birds took toll of the ducks'
eggs and ducklings when they had a nest full of
ravenous young to feed, it was resolved that
they should no longer be tolerated ; their nests
were ordered to be pulled down and the old
birds shot whenever an opportunity offered.
Now it is not the Hyde Park crows alone that
will suffer if this policy be adhered to, but the
London crows generally will be in danger of

extermination, for the birds are constantly
passing and repassing across London, visiting
all the parks where there are large trees, on
their way to and from their various feeding-
grounds. Hyde Park with Kensington Gardens
is one of their favourite stopping places ; one or
more pairs may be seen there on most mornings,
frequently at noon again on their return to
Richmond, Kew, and Syon Park, and to the
northern heights of London. On the morning
of October 10, 1896, I saw eight carrion crows,
in pairs, perched at a considerable distance apart
on the elm-tops near the palace in Kensington
Gardens. After calling for some time on the
trees, they began to pursue and buffet one
another with violence, making the whole place
in the meantime resound with their powerful,
harsh, grating cries. Their mock battle over,
they rose to a considerable height in the air
and went away towards Hammersmith It
seemed to me a marvellous thing that I had
witnessed such a scene in such a place. But it
is not necessary to see a number of carrion
crows together to feel impressed with the
appearance of the bird. There are few finer
sights in the wild bird life of London than one

of these visitors to the park on any autumn or
winter morning, when he will allow you to come
quite near to the leafless tree on which he is
perched, to stand still and admire his massive
raven-like beak and intense black plumage
glossed with metallic green, as he sits flirting
his wings and tail, swelling his throat to the size
of a duck's egg, as, at intervals, he pours out a
succession of raucous caws—the cry of a true
savage, and the crow's ' voice of care,' as
Chaucer called it.

The crow is, in fact, the grandest wild bird
left to us in the metropolis ; and after corresponding and conversing with a large number
of persons on the subject, I find that in London
others—most persons, I believe—admire him as
much as I do, and are just as anxious that he
should be preserved.   It may be mentioned here
that in two or three of the County Council's
parks the superintendents protect and take pride
in their crows.   Why, then, should these few
birds, which Londoners value, be destroyed in the
royal parks for fear of the loss of a few ducklings
out of the hundreds that are annually hatched
and reared ?

The   ducks   in   the   Serpentine   are   very

numerous ; many bucketfuls of food—meal and grain—are given to them every day when they congregate at the boat-house, and they get besides large quantities of broken bread cast to them by the public ; all day long, and every day when it is not raining, there is a continual procession of men, women, and children bringing food for the birds. Is it permissible to ask for whose advantage this large number of ducks is reared and fattened for the table at so small a cost ? Hyde Park is maintained by the nation, and presumably for the nation ; it is a national as well as a royal park ; is it not extraordinary that so noble a possession, the largest and most beautiful open space in the capital of the British empire, the chief city of the world, should be degraded to something like a poultry farm, or at all events a duck-breeding establishment, and that in order to get as much profit as possible out of the ducks, one of the chief ornaments of the park, the one representative of noble wild bird life that has survived until now in London, should be sacrificed ?

Let us by all means have ducks, and many of them ; they are gregarious by nature and look well in flocks, and are a source of innocent pleasure to numberless visitors to the parks, especially to children and nursemaids ; but let us not have ducks only—a great multitude of ducks, to the exclusion of other wilder and nobler birds.

Personally, I am very fond of these ducks, although I have never had one on my table, and believe that I am as well able to appreciate their beauty and feel an interest in their habits as any of the gentlemen in authority who have decreed that the carrion crow shall go the way of the raven in Hyde Park. I love them because they are not the ducks that have been made lazy and fat, with all their fine faculties dulled, by long domestication. They are the wild duck, or mallard, introduced many years ago into the Serpentine. Doubtless they have some domestic taint in them, since the young birds reared each season exhibit a very considerable variation in colour and markings. Those that vary in colour are weeded out each winter, and the original type is in this way preserved ; but not strictly preserved, as the weeding-out process is carelessly—I had almost said stupidly—performed.

The thinning takes place in December, and at

'THE SEVEN SISTERS'

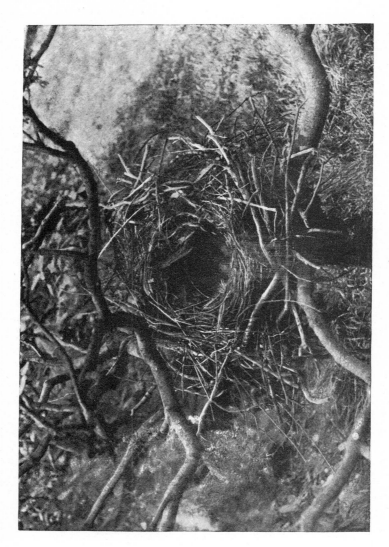

CARRION CROW'S NEST

that season people who live in the vicinity of the park are startled each morning by the sound of firing, as at the covert side. The sub-ranger and his friends and underlings are enjoying their big annual shoot. And there is no reason why they should not have this sport, if it pleases them, and if by this means the object sought could be obtained. But it is not obtained, as anyone may see for himself; and it also seems a trifle ridiculous that any man can find sport in shooting birds accustomed to walk about among people's legs and feed out of little children's hands.

Once upon a time, in a distant country, I came with a companion to a small farmhouse. We were very much in want of a meal, but no person was about, and the larder was empty, and so we determined to kill and broil a chicken for ourselves. On our making certain chuckling noises, which domestic birds understand, a number of fowls scattered about near the place rushed up to us, expecting to be fed. We made choice of a very tall cockerel for our breakfast ; so tall was this young bird on his long, bright yellow stilt-like shanks that he towered head and neck above his fellows. My companion,

who was an American, had a revolver in his
pocket, and pulling it out he fired five shots at
the bird at a distance of about six yards, but
failed to hit it.   He was preparing to reload his
weapon, when, to expedite matters, I picked up
a stick and knocked the chicken over, and in
less than fifty minutes' time we were picking his
bones.

I doubt if the Hyde Park sportsmen will see
anything very amusing in this story.

The mallard is an extremely handsome
fowl, and it is pleasant to see such a bird in
flocks, at home on the ornamental waters, and
at the same time to learn that it is, in a sense, a
wild bird, that in the keenness of its faculties,
its power of flight, and nesting habits it differs
greatly from its degenerate domestic relation.
By day he will feed from any person's hand ;
in the evening he returns to his ancient wary
habit, and will not suffer a person to approach
him.   He is active by night, particularly in the
autumn, flying about the park and gardens in
small flocks and feeding on the grass.   It is a
curious and delightful experience to be alone on
a damp autumn night in Kensington Gardens.
One is surrounded by London ; its dull con-

tinuous murmur may be heard, and the glinting of distant lamps catches the eye through the trees ; these fitful gleams and distant sounds but make the silence and darkness all the more deep and impressive. Suddenly the whistling of wings is heard, and the loud startled cry of a mallard, as the birds, vaguely seen, rush by overhead ; the effect on the mind is wonderful—one has been transported as by a miracle into the midst of a wild and solitary nature.

Both by day and night there is much going to and fro between the Serpentine and the Round Pond, but each bird appears to be faithful to its *home*, and those that have been reared on the Round Pond breed in its vicinity on the west side of the gardens. Where their eggs are deposited is known to few. Strange as it may seem, they nest in the trees, in holes in the trunks of the large elms, in many cases at a height of thirty feet or more from the ground. Some of the breeding-trees are known, of others the secret has been well kept by the birds. Not a few ducks breed in Holland Park, and find it an exceedingly difficult matter to get their broods into the gardens. More than once the strange spectacle of a duck leading its newly-

hatched young along the thronged pavements
of Kensington High Street has been witnessed.

When the young have been hatched in a tree
the parent bird takes them up in her beak and
drops them one by one to the ground, and the
fall does not appear to hurt them.   Last year a
duck bred in a tree broken off at the top near
St. Gover's Well, in the gardens.   One morning
she appeared with four ducklings, and leaving
them near the pond went back to the tree and
in time returned with a second lot of four.   Still
she was not satisfied, but continued to go back
to the tree and to fly round and round it with a
great clamour.   A keeper who had been watching
her movements sent for a man with a ladder to
have the tree-top examined.   The man found
the broken stem hollow at the top, and by
thrusting his arm down shoulder-deep was able
to reach the bottom of the cavity with his hand.
One duckling was found in it and rescued, and
its mother made happy.   That she had succeeded in getting all the others out of so
deep and narrow a shaft seemed very astonishing.

An extraordinary incident relating to these
Kensington ducks was told to me by one of the

keepers, who himself heard it by a very curious chance. One dark evening, after leaving the gardens, he got on to an omnibus near the Albert Hall to go to his home at Hammersmith. Two men who occupied the seat in front of him were talking about the gardens and the birds, and he listened. One of the men related that he once succeeded in taking a clutch of ducks' eggs from the gardens. He put them under a hen at his home in Hammersmith, and nine ducklings were hatched. They were healthy and strong and grew up into nine as fine ducks as he had ever seen. Such fine birds were they that he was loth to kill or part with them, and before he had made up his mind what to do he lost them in a very strange way. One morning he was in his back yard, where his birds were kept, when a crow appeared flying by at a considerable height in the air; instantly the ducks, with raised heads, ran together, then with a scream of terror sprang into the air and flew away, to be seen no more. Up till that moment they had never seen beyond the small back yard where they lived—it was their world—nor had any one of them ever attempted to use his wings.

Let us now return to the nobler bird, the subject of this chapter.

It would not, I imagine, be difficult for one who had the time to count the London crows; those I am accustomed to see number about twenty, and I should not be surprised to learn that as many as forty crows frequent inner London. But with the exception of two, or perhaps three pairs, they do not now breed in London, but have their nesting-haunts in woods west, north, and east of the metropolis. These breeders on the outskirts bring the young they succeed in rearing to the parks, from which they have themselves in some cases been expelled, and the tradition is thus kept up. Most of the birds appear to fly over London every day, paying long visits on their way to Regent's Park, Holland Park, the central parks, and Battersea Park. As their movements are very regular it would be possible to mark their various routes on a map of the metropolis.

Mr. W. H. Tuck, writing to me about the carrion crow, says: ' For many years, when living in Kensington, several pairs of crows going from N.E. to S.W. passed at daybreak over my house on their way to the Thames banks at Chelsea, and I could always time them within a minute or two.' These birds come on their way from the northern heights to the river at Chelsea; the crows that breed in the neighbourhood of Syon Park and Richmond fly over the central parks to Westminster, and then follow the river down to its mouth.

The persistency with which the carrion crow keeps to his nesting-place may be seen in the case of a pair that have bred in private grounds at Hillfield, Hampstead, for at least sixty years. Nor is it impossible to believe that the same birds have occupied the site for this long period, the crow being a long-lived creature. The venerable author of 'Festus,' who also has the secret of long life, might have been thinking of this very pair when, more than half a century ago, he wrote his spirited lyric :—

> The crow ! the crow ! the great black crow !
> He lives for a hundred years and mo' ;
> He lives till he dies, and he dies as slow
> As the morning mists down the hill that go.
> Go—go ! you great black crow !
> But it's fine to live and die like a great black crow.

Many persons might be inclined to think that it must be better for the crow to have his

nest a little way out of the hurly-burly, or at
all events within easy reach of the country;
for how, they might ask, can this large flesh-
eating, voracious creature feed himself and rear
a nest full of young with cormorant appetites in
London?

Eliza Cook, whose now universally neglected
works I admired as a boy, makes the bird say,
in her 'Song of the Crow':—

> I plunged my beak in the marbling cheek,
> I perched on the clammy brow;
> And a dainty treat was that fresh meat
> To the greedy carrion crow.

The unknown author of 'The Twa Corbies'
was a better naturalist as well as a better poet
when he wrote—

> I'll pick out his bonny blue een.

But this relates to a time when the bodies of
dead men, as well as of other large animals,
were left lying promiscuously about; in these
ultra-civilised days, when all dead things are
quickly and decently interred, the greedy carrion
crow has greatly modified his feeding habits.
In London, as in most places, he takes whatever
he finds on the table, and though not in principle

a vegetarian, there is no doubt that he feeds largely on vegetable substances. Like the sparrow and other London birds, he has become with us a great bread-eater.

Mr. Kempshall, the superintendent at Clissold Park, relates a curious story of this civilised taste in the crow. The park for very many years was the home of a pair of these birds. Unfortunately, when this space was opened to the public, in 1889, the birds forsook it, and settled in some large trees on private grounds in the neighbourhood. These trees were cut down about three years ago, whereupon the birds returned to Clissold Park; but they have now again left it. One summer morning before the park was opened, when there were young crows in the nest, Mr. Kempshall observed one of the old birds laboriously making his way across the open ground towards the nesting-tree, laden with a strange-looking object. This was white and round and three times as big as an orange, and the crow, flying close to the ground, was obliged to alight at short intervals, whereupon he would drop his pack and take a rest. Curious to know what he was carrying, the superintendent made a sudden rush at the

bird, at a moment when he had set his burden
down, and succeeded in getting near enough to
see that the white object was the round top
part of a cottage loaf. But though the rush had
been sudden and unexpected, and accompanied
with a startling shout, the crow did not lose his
head ; striking his powerful beak, or *plunging* it,
as Eliza Cook would have said, into the mass, he
flopped up and struggled resolutely on until he
reached the nest, to be boisterously welcomed
by his hungry family. They had a big meal,
but perhaps grumbled a little at so much bread
without any ghee.

Probably the London crows get most of their
food from the river. Very early every morning,
as we have seen, they wing their way to the
Thames, and at all hours of the day, when not
engaged in breeding, crows may be seen travelling up and down the river, usually in couples,
from Barnes and Mortlake and higher up, down
to the sea. They search the mud at low tide
for dead fishes, garbage, bread, and vegetable
matter left by the water. Even when the tide
is at its full the birds are still able to pick up
something to eat, as they have borrowed the
gull's habit of dropping upon the water to pick

up any floating object which may form part of their exceedingly varied dietary. It is amusing to see the carrion crow fishing up his dinner in this way, for he does not venture to fold his wings like the gull and examine and take up the morsel at leisure ; he drops upon the water rather awkwardly, wetting his legs and belly, but keeps working his wings until he has secured the floating object, then rises heavily with it in his beak. Another curious habit of some London crows in the south-west district, is to alight, dove-like, on the roofs and chimney-stacks of tall houses.

In an article on this bird which appeared in the ' Fortnightly Review ' for May 1895, I wrote : ' It sometimes greatly adds to our knowledge of any wild creature to see it tamed—not confined in any way, nor with its wings clipped, but free to exercise all its faculties and to come and go at will. Some species in this condition are very much more companionable than others, and probably none so readily fall into the domestic life as the various members of the crow family ; for they are more intelligent and adaptive, and nearer to the mammalians in their mental character than most birds. It is therefore curious to find that the subject of this paper appears to be little known as a domestic bird, or pet. A caged crow, being next door, so to speak, to a dead and stuffed crow, does not interest me. Yet the crow strikes one as a bird with great possibilities as a pet : one would like to observe him freely associating with the larger unfeathered crows that have a different language, to learn by what means he communicates with them, to sound his depths of amusing devilry, and note the modulations of his voice ; for he, too, like other corvines, is loquacious on occasions, and much given to soliloquy. He is also a musician, a fact which is referred to by Æsop, Yarrell, and other authorities, but they have given us no proper description of his song. A friend tells me that he once kept a crow which did not prove a very interesting pet. This was not strange in the circumstances. The bird was an old one, just knocked down with a charge of shot, when he was handed over in a dazed condition to my informant. He recovered from his wounds, but was always a very sedate bird. He had the run of a big old country house, and was one day observed in a crouching attitude pressed tightly into the angle formed by the wall and floor. He had discovered that the place was infested by mice, and was watching a crevice. The instant that a mouse put out a head the crow had him in his beak, and would kill him by striking him with lightning rapidity two or three times on the floor, then swallow him. From that time mouse-catching was this bird's sole occupation and amusement, and he went about the house in the silent and stealthy manner of a cat.

' I am anxious to get the history of a tame crow that never had his wing-feathers clipped, and did not begin the domestic life as an old bird with several pellets of lead in his body.'

Curiously enough, not long after this article appeared another bird-lover in London was asking the same question in another journal. This was Mr. Mandeville B. Phillips, of South Norwood, then private secretary to the late Archbishop of Canterbury. By accident he had become possessed of a carrion crow, sold to him as a young raven taken from a nest at Ely. This bird made so interesting a pet that its owner became desirous of hearing the experiences of others who had kept carrion crows. Mr. Phillips, in kindly giving me the history of his bird, says that at different times he has kept ravens, daws, jays, and magpies, but has never had so delightful a bird friend as the crow. It was a revelation to him to find what an interesting pet this species made. No other bird he had owned approached him in cleverness and in multiplicity of tricks and devices : he could give the cleverest jackdaw points and win easily. If his bird was an average specimen of the race, he wondered that the crow is not more popular as a pet. This bird was fond of his liberty, but would always come to his master when called, and roosted every night in an outhouse. Like the tame raven, and also like human beings of a primitive order of mind, he was excessively fond of practical jokes, and whenever he found the dog or cat asleep he would steal quietly up and administer a severe prod on the tail with his powerful beak. He would also fly into the kitchen when he saw the window open, to steal the spoons ; but his chief delight was in a box of matches, which he would carry off to pick to pieces and scatter the matches all over the place. He was extremely jealous of a tame raven and a jackdaw that shared the house and garden with him, and which he chose to regard as rivals ; but this was his only unhappiness. The appearance of his master dressed in ' blazers ' always greatly affected him. It would, indeed, throw him into such a frenzy of terror that Mr. Phillips became careful not to exhibit himself in such bizarre raiment in the garden. My informant concludes, that he is not ashamed to say that he shed a few tears at the loss of this bird.

I may add that I received a large number of letters in answer to my article on the carrion crow, but none of my correspondents in this country had any knowledge of the bird as a pet. In several letters received from America—the States and Canada—long histories of the common crow of that region as a pet bird were sent to me.

CHAPTER IV

THE LONDON DAW

Rarity of the daw in London—Pigeons and daws compared—
Æsthetic value of the daw as a cathedral bird—Kensington
Palace daws ; their disposition and habits—Friendship with
rooks—Wandering daws at Clissold Park—Solitary daws—
Mr. Mark Melford's birds—Rescue of a hundred daws—The
strange history of an egg-stealing daw—White daws—White
ravens—Willughby's speculations—A suggestion.

IT is somewhat curious to find that the jackdaw
is an extremely rare bird in London—that, in
fact, with the exception of a small colony at one
spot, he is almost non-existent.   At Richmond
Park, where pheasants (and the gamekeeper's
traditions) are preserved, he was sometimes shot
in the breeding season ; but in the metropolis,
so far as I know, he has never been persecuted.
Yet there are few birds, certainly no member of
the crow family, seemingly so well adapted to a
London life as this species.   Throughout the
kingdom he is a familiar town bird ; in one
English cathedral over a hundred pairs have

PIGEONS AT THE LAW COURTS

WOOD-PIGEON ON SHAKESPEARE'S STATUE

their nests ; and in that city and in many other
towns the birds are accustomed to come to the
gardens and window-sills, to be fed on scraps
by their human neighbours and friends.

While the daw has diminished with us, and
is near to vanishing, the common pigeon—the
domestic variety of the blue rock—has increased
excessively in recent years. Large colonies of
these birds inhabit the Temple Gardens, the Law
Courts, St. Paul's, the Museum, and Westminster
Palace, and many smaller settlements exist all over
the metropolis. Now, a flock or cloud of parti-
coloured pigeons rushing up and wheeling about
the roofs or fronts of these imposing structures
forms a very pretty sight ; but the daw toying
with the wind, that lifts and blows him hither
and thither, is a much more engaging spectacle,
and in London we miss him greatly.

I have often thought that it was due to the
presence of the daw that I was ever able to get
an adequate or satisfactory idea of the beauty
and grandeur of some of our finest buildings.
Watching the bird in his aërial evolutions, now
suspended motionless, or rising and falling, then
with half-closed wings precipitating himself
downwards, as if demented, through vast

distances, only to mount again with an exulting
cry, to soar beyond the highest tower or pinnacle,
and seem at that vast height no bigger than a
swift in size—watching him thus, an image of
the structure over and around which he disported
himself so gloriously has been formed—its vastness, stability, and perfect proportions—and has
remained thereafter a vivid picture in my mind.
How much would be lost to the sculptured
west front of Wells Cathedral, the soaring spire
of Salisbury, the noble roof and towers of York
Minster and of Canterbury, if the jackdaws
were not there! I know that, compared with
the images I retain of many daw-haunted cathedrals and castles in the provinces, those of the
cathedrals and other great buildings in London
have in my mind a somewhat dim and blurred
appearance. It is a pity that, before consenting
to rebuild St. Paul's Cathedral, Sir Christopher
Wren did not make the perpetual maintenance
of a colony of jackdaws a condition. And if he
had bargained with posterity for a pair or two
of peregrine falcons and kestrels, his glory at the
present time would have been greater.

There are, I believe, about sixteen hundred
churches in London; probably not more than

three are now tenanted by the ' ecclesiastical daw.'

On the borders of London—at Hampstead, Greenwich, Dulwich, Richmond, and other points —daws in limited numbers are to be met with; in London proper, or inner London, there are no resident or breeding daws except the small colony of about twenty-four birds at Kensington Palace. Most of these breed in the hollow elms in Kensington Gardens; others in trees in Holland Park. There is something curious about this small isolated colony: the birds are far less loquacious and more sedate in manner than daws are wont to be. At almost any hour of the day they may be seen sitting quietly on the higher branches of the tall trees, silent and spiritless. The wind blows, and they rise not to play with it; the graceful spire of St. Mary Abbott's springs high above the garden trees and palace and neighbouring buildings, but it does not attract them. Occasionally, in winter, when the morning sun shines bright and melts the mist, they experience a sudden return of the old frolicsome mood, and at such moments are capable of a very fine display, rushing over and among the tall elms in a black train, yelping

like a pack of aërial hounds in hot pursuit of
some invisible quarry.

A still greater excitement is exhibited by
these somewhat depressed and sedentary Kensington birds on the appearance of a flight of
rooks ; for rooks, sometimes in considerable
numbers, do occasionally visit or pass over
London, and keep, when travelling east or west,
to the wide green way of the central parks.
Now there are few more impressive spectacles in
bird life in this country than the approach of a
large company of rooks ; their black forms, that
loom so large as they successively appear, follow
each other with slow deliberate motion at long
intervals, moving as in a funeral procession, with
appropriate solemn noises, which may be heard
when they are still at a great distance.   They
are chanting something that corresponds in the
corvine world to our Dead March in ' Saul.'
The coming sound has a magical effect on the
daws ; their answering cries ring out loud and
sharp, and hurriedly mounting to a considerable
height in the air, they go out to meet the pro-
cessionists, to mix with and accompany them a
distance on the journey.   It is to me a wonderful
sight—more   wonderful   here   in   Kensington

Gardens, which have long been rookless, than in
any country place, and has reminded me of the
meeting of two savage tribes or families, living
far apart but cherishing an ancient tradition of
kinship and amity, who, after a long interval,
perhaps of years, when at last they come in
sight of each other's faces rush together, bursting
into loud shouts of greeting and welcome. And
one is really inclined to believe at times that
some such traditional alliance and feeling of
friendship exists between these two most social
and human-like of the crow family.

Besides this small remnant of birds native to
London, flocks of jackdaws from outside occasionally appear when migrating or in search of
new quarters. One morning, not long ago, a
flock of fifteen came down at Clissold Park.
They settled on the dovecote, and amused themselves in a characteristic way by hunting the
pigeons out of their boxes ; then, having cleared
the place, they remained contentedly for an hour
or two, dozing, preening their feathers, and
conversing together in low tones. The bird-
loving superintendent's heart was filled with joy
at the acquisition of so interesting a colony ;
but his rejoicing was premature, the loud call

and invitation to fly was at last sounded, and
hastily responded to—*We have not come to stay—
we are off — good-bye — so-long—farewell*—and
forthwith they rose up and flew away, probably
in search of fresher woods and less trodden
pastures than those of Clissold Park.

There are also to be met with in London a
few solitary vagrant daws which in most cases
are probably birds escaped from captivity.
Close to my home a daw of this description
appears every morning at the house of a friend
and demands his breakfast with loud taps on the
window-pane. The generous treatment he has
received has caused him to abandon his first
suspicious attitude ; he now flies boldly into the
house and explores the rooms, and is specially
interested in the objects on the dressing-table.
Articles of jewellery are carefully put out of sight
when he makes a call.

My friends, Mr. and Mrs. Mark Melford, of
Fulham, are probably responsible for the existence in London of a good number of wandering
solitary jackdaws. They cherish a wonderful
admiration and affection towards all the members of the crow family, and have had numberless daws, jays, and pies as pets, or rather

as guests, since their birds are always free to fly about the house and go and come at pleasure. But their special favourite is the daw, which they regard as far more intelligent, interesting, and companionable than any other animal, not excepting the dog. On one occasion Mr. Melford saw an advertisement of a hundred daws to be sold for trap-shooting, and to save them from so miserable a fate he at once purchased the lot and took them home. They were in a miserable half-starved condition, and to give them a better chance of survival, before freeing them he placed them in an outhouse in his garden with a wire-netting across the doorway, and there he fed and tended them until they were well and strong, and then gave them their liberty. But they did not at once take advantage of it; grown used to the place and the kindly faces of their protectors, they remained and were like tame birds about the house; but later, a few at a time, at long intervals, they went away and back to their wild independent life.

Of the many stories of their pet daws which they have told me, I will give one of a bird which was a particular favourite of Mrs. Melford's.

His invariable habit was, on returning from an
expedition abroad, to fly straight into the house
in search of her, and, sitting on her head, to

THE LADY AND THE DAW

express his affection and delight at rejoining her
by passing his beak through her hair.

Unfortunately, this bird had a weakness for

eggs, which led him into many scrapes, and in
the end very nearly proved his undoing. He
was constantly hanging about and prying into
the fowl-house, and whenever he felt sure that
he was not observed he would slip in to purloin
an egg. His cunning reacted on the fowls and
made them cunning too. When he appeared
they looked the other way, or walked off pre-
tending not to see him; but no sooner would he
be inside exploring the obscure corners for an
egg than the battle-cry would sound, and then
poor Jackie would find it hard indeed to escape
from their fury with nothing worse than a sound
drubbing. In a day or two, before his many
sores and bruises had had time to heal, the
cackling of a hen and the thought of a new-laid
egg would tempt him again, and at length one
day he could not escape; the loud cries of rage
and of vengeance gratified attracted some person
to the fowl-house, where Jackie was found lying
on the ground in the midst of a crowd of fowls
engaged in pounding and pecking his life out,
scattering his hated black feathers in all directions He was rescued more dead than alive,
and subsequently tended by his mistress with
loving care. He lived, but failed to recover

his old gay spirits; day after day he moped
in silence, a picture of abject misery, recalling
in his half-naked, bruised, and bedraggled appearance the famous bird of Rheims, the stealer
of the turquoise ring, after the awful malediction
of the Lord Cardinal Archbishop had taken effect:

> On crumpled claw,
> Came limping a poor little lame jackdaw,
> No longer gay
> As on yesterday;
> His feathers all seemed to be turned the wrong way;
> His pinions drooped, he could hardly stand,
> His head was as bald as the palm of your hand;
> His eye so dim,
> So wasted each limb,
> That, heedless of grammar, they all cried ' That's
> him!'

By-and-by, when still in this broken-hearted
and broken-feathered state, a sight to make his
mistress weep, he disappeared; it was conjectured that some compassionate-minded neighbour, finding him in his garden or grounds, and
seeing his pitiable condition, had put an end to
his misery.

One day, a year later, Mrs. Melford, who
was just recovering from an illness, was lying

on a sofa in a room on the ground floor, when
her husband, who was in the garden at the back,
excitedly cried out that a wild jackdaw had just
flown down and alighted near him. ' A perfect
beauty!' he exclaimed ; never had he seen a jackdaw in finer plumage ! The lady, equally excited,
called back, begging him to use every device to
get the bird to stay. No sooner was her voice
heard than the jackdaw rose up and dashed into
the house, and flying the length of three rooms
came to where she was lying, and at once
alighted on her head and began passing his
beak through her hair in the old manner. In
no other way could this wild-looking and
beautified bird have established his identity.
His return was a great joy ; they caressed and
feasted him, and for several hours, during which
he showed no desire to renew his intercourse
with the fowls, he was as lively and amusing
as he had ever been in the old days before he
had got into trouble. But before night he left
them, and has never returned since ; doubtless
he had established relations with some of the wild
daws on the outskirts of London.

Before ending this chapter I should like to
say a word about white jackdaws. It is a

mystery to me where all the albinos occasionally to be seen in the London bird markets
come from. I have seen half a dozen in the
hands of one large dealer, two at another
dealer's, and several single birds at other shops ;
altogether about sixteen or eighteen white daws
on sale at one time.

One often hears of and occasionally sees a
white blackbird or other species in a wild state,
but these uncoloured specimens are rare ; they
are also dear to the collector (nobody knows
why), and as a rule are not long permitted to
enjoy existence. Besides, in nine cases out of
ten the abnormally white birds are not albinos.
They are probably mere ' sports,' like our
domestic white pigeons, fowls, and ducks, and
would doubtless be more common but for the
fact that their whiteness is a disadvantage to
them in their struggle for life. It is rather
curious to find that among wild birds those that
have a black plumage appear more subject to
loss of colour than others. Thus we find that,
of our small birds, whiteness is more common
in the blackbird than in any other species.
Within the last twelve to eighteen months I have
known of the existence of seven or eight white

or partly white blackbirds in London ; but during the same period I have not seen nor heard of a white thrush, and have only seen one white sparrow. My belief is that the species most commonly found with white or partly white plumage are the blackbird, rook, and daw. When carrion crows and ravens were abundant in this country it was probably no very unusual thing to meet with white specimens. The old ornithologist, Willughby, writing over two centuries ago, mentions two milk-white ravens which he saw ; but the fact of their whiteness is less interesting to read at this distant date than the old author's delightful speculations as to the cause of the phenomenon. He doubts that white ravens were as common in this country as Aldrovandus had affirmed that they were, and then adds : ' I rather think that they are found in those mountainous Northern Countries, which are for the greatest part of the year covered with snow : Where also many other Animals change their native colours, and become white, as *Bears, Foxes, Blackbirds,* &c., whether it proceeds from the force of imagi-nation, heightened by the constant intuition of Snow, or from the cold of the Climate, occasion-

ing such a languishing of colour ; as we see in old
Age, when the natural heat decays, the hair
grows grey, and at last white.'

To return to the subject of the beautiful
albino daws, and the numbers sometimes seen in
our bird markets. One can only say that the
monster London throws its nets over an
exceedingly wide area, capturing all rare and
quaint and beautiful things for its own delight.
Thinking of these wonderful white daws, when
I have cast up my eyes to the birdless towers
and domes of our great London buildings, it has
occurred to me to ask the following question :
Is there not one among the many very wealthy
men in London, who annually throw away
hundreds of thousands of pounds on their
several crazes—is there not one to give, say,
fifty or sixty pounds per annum to buy up all
these beautiful albinos, at the usual price of
one or two guineas per bird, for three or four
years, and establish a colony at Westminster, or
other suitable place, where thousands of people
would have great delight in looking at them
every day ? For it would indeed be a strange
and beautiful sight, and many persons would

come from a distance solely to see the milk-
white daws soaring in the wind, as their custom
is, above the roofs and towers ; and he who
made such a gift to London would be long and
very pleasantly remembered.

CHAPTER V

EXPULSION OF THE ROOKS

Positions of the rook and crow compared—Gray's Inn Gardens rookery—Break-up of the old, and futile attempt of the birds to establish new rookeries—The rooks a great loss to London—Why the rook is esteemed—Incidents in the life of a tame rook—A first sight of the Kensington Gardens rookery—The true history of the expulsion of the rooks—A desolate scene, and a vision of London beautified.

WE have seen how it is with the carrion crow—that he is in the balance, and that if the park authorities will but refrain from persecuting him he will probably be able to keep his ancient place among the wild birds of London. To what has already been said on the subject of this bird I will only add here that there is, just now, an unfortunate inclination in some of the County Council's parks to adopt the policy of the royal parks—to set too high a value on domestic and ornamental water-fowl, which, however beautiful and costly they may be, can never give as much pleasure or produce

the same effect on the mind as the wild bird.
The old London crow is worth more to London
than many exotic swans and ducks and geese.

We have also seen that the case of the jack-

LONDON CROWS

daw is not quite hopeless; for although the
birds are now reduced to an insignificant
remnant, the habits and disposition of this
species make it reasonable to hope that they

will thrive and increase, and, in any case, that
if we want the daw we can have him. But the
case of the rook appears to me well nigh hopeless, and on this account, in this list of the
corvines, he is put last that should have been
first. There are nevertheless two reasons why a
considerable space—a whole chapter—should be
given to this species : one is, that down to
within a few years ago the rook attracted the
largest share of attention, and was the most
important species in the wild bird life of the
metropolis ; the other, that it would be well that
the cause of its departure should not be forgotten.
It is true that in the very heart of the metropolis
a rookery still exists in Gray's Inn Gardens, and
that although it does not increase neither does
it diminish. Thus, during the last twenty years
there have never been fewer than seventeen or
eighteen, and never more than thirty nests in a
season ; and for the last three seasons the numbers have been twenty-five, twenty-three, and
twenty-four nests. Going a little farther back
in the history of this ancient famous colony, it
is well to relate that, twenty-three years ago, it
was well-nigh lost for ever through an uncon-
sidered act of the Benchers, or of some ignorant

person in authority among them. It was thought that the trees would have a better appearance if a number of their large horizontal branches were lopped off, and the work was carried out in the month of March, just when the rooks were busy repairing their old and building new nests. The birds were seized with panic, and went away in a body to be seen no more for the space of three years ; then they returned to settle once more, and at present they are regarded with so much pride and affection by the Benchers, and have so much food cast to them out of scores of windows, that they have grown to be the most domestic and stay-at-home rooks to be found anywhere in England.

With the exception of this one small colony, it is sad to have to say that utter, irretrievable disaster has fallen on the inner London rookeries —those that still exist in the suburbs will be mentioned in subsequent chapters—and although rooks may still be found within our gates, go they will and go they must, never to return. The few birds that continue in constantly diminishing numbers to breed here and there in the metropolis, in spite of its gloomy atmosphere and the long distances they are obliged

to travel in quest of grubs and worms for
their young, are London rooks, themselves
hatched in parks and squares—the town has
always been their home and breeding place ; and
although it is more than probable that some of
these town birds are from time to time enticed
away to the country, it is indeed hard to believe
that rooks hatched in the rural districts are ever
tempted to come to us.   During the last dozen
years many attempts at founding new colonies
have been made by small bands of rooks.   These
birds were and are survivors of the old broken-
up communities.   All these incipient rookeries,
containing from two or three to a dozen nests
(as at Connaught Square), have failed ; but the
birds, or some of them, still wander about in an
aimless way in small companies, from park to
park, and there is no doubt that year by year
these homeless rooks will continue to decrease
in number, until the ancient tradition is lost,
and they will be seen no more.

It is no slight loss which we have to lament ;
it is the loss to the millions inhabiting this city,
or congeries of cities and towns, of a bird which
is more to us than any other wild bird, on
account of its large size and interesting social

habits, its high intelligence, and the confidence
it reposes in man ; and, finally, of that ancient
kindly regard and pride in it which, in some
degree, is felt by all persons throughout the
kingdom. The rook has other claims to our
esteem and affection which are not so generally
known : in a domestic state it is no whit behind other species in the capacity for strong
attachments, in versatility and playfulness, and
that tricksy spirit found in most of the corvines,
which so curiously resembles, or simulates, the
sense of humour in ourselves.

I recall here an incident in the life of a tame
rook, and by way of apology for introducing it
I may mention that this bird, although country
bred, was of London too, when his mistress
came to town for the season accompanied by
her glossy black pet. I will first relate something of his country life, and feel confident that
this digression will be pardoned by those of my
readers who are admirers of the rook, a bird
which we are accustomed to regard as of a more
sedate disposition than the jackdaw.

He was picked up injured in a park in
Oxfordshire, taken in and nursed by the lady
of the house until he was well and able to fly

about once more ; but he elected to stay with
his benefactress, although he always spent a
portion of each day in flying about the country
in company with his fellows. He had various
ways of showing his partiality for his mistress,
one of which was very curious. Early every
morning he flew into her bedroom by the open
window, and alighting on her bed would deposit
a small offering on the pillow—a horse-chestnut
bur, a little crooked stick, a bleached rabbit
bone, a pebble, a bit of rusty iron, which he
had picked up and regarded as a suitable
present. Whatever it was, it had to be accepted
with demonstrations of gratitude and affection.
If she took no notice he would lift it up and
replace it again, calling attention to it with
little subdued exclamations which sounded like
words, and if she feigned sleep he would gently
pull her hair or tap her cheek with his bill to
awake her. Once the present was accepted he
would nestle in under her arm and remain so,
very contentedly, until she got up.

Here we get a delightful little peep into the
workings of the rook's mind. We ourselves,
our great philosopher tells us, are ' hopelessly '
anthropomorphic. The rook appears to be in as

bad a case; to his mind we are nothing but bigger rooks, somewhat misshapen, perhaps, featherless, deprived by some accident of the faculty of flight, and not very well able to take care of ourselves.

One summer day the rook came into the daughter's bedroom, where she was washing her hands, and had just taken off a valuable diamond ring from her finger and placed it on the marble top of the washing-stand. The rook came to the stand and very suddenly picked up the ring and flew out at the open window. The young lady ran down stairs and on to the terrace, calling out that the bird had flown away with her ring. Her mother quickly came out with a field glass in her hand, and together they watched the bird fly straight away across the park to a distance of about a third of a mile, where he disappeared from sight among the trees. The ring was gone! Two hours later the robber returned and flew into the dining-room, where his mistress happened to be; alighting on the table, he dropped the ring from his beak and began walking round it, viewing it first with one, then the other eye, uttering the while a variety of little complacent notes, in which he seemed to

be saying: ' I have often admired this beautiful
ring, but never had an opportunity of examining
it properly before ; now, after having had it for
some time in my possession and shown it to
several wild rooks of my acquaintance, I have
much satisfaction in restoring it to its owner,
who is my very good friend.'

During his summer visits to London this
rook met with many curious and amusing
adventures, as he had the habit of flying in at
the open windows of houses in the neighbourhood of Park Lane, and making himself very
much at home. He also flew about Hyde Park
and Kensington Gardens every day to visit his
fellow-rooks. One day his mistress was walking
in the Row, at an hour when it was full of
fashionable people, and the rook, winging his
way homewards from the gardens, spied her,
and circling down alighted on her shoulders, to
the amazement of all who witnessed the incident.
' What an astonishing thing ! ' exclaimed some
person in the crowd that gathered round her.
' Oh, not at all,' answered the lady, caressing
the bird with her hand, while he rubbed his
beak against her cheek ; ' if you were as fond of
the birds as I am, and treated them as well,

they would be glad to come down on to your shoulders, too.'

This happened when the now vanished rooks had their populous rookery in Kensington Gardens, where they were to be seen all day flying to and from the old nesting-trees, and stalking over the green turf in search of grubs on the open portions of Hyde Park. And we should have had them there now if they had not been driven out.

The two largest London rookeries were those at Greenwich Park and Kensington Gardens. In the first-named the trees were all topped over twenty years ago, with the result that the birds left; and although the locality has much to attract them, and numbers of rooks constantly visit the park, they have never attempted to build nests since the trees were mutilated. This rookery I never saw; that of Kensington Gardens I knew very well.

Over twenty years ago, on arriving in London, I put up at a City hotel, and on the following day went out to explore, and walked at random, never inquiring my way of any person, and not knowing whether I was going

east or west.   After rambling about for some
three or four hours, I came to a vast wooded
place where few persons were about.   It was a
wet, cold morning in early May, after a night
of incessant rain ; but when I reached this
unknown place the sun shone out and made the
air warm and fragrant and the grass and trees
sparkle with innumerable raindrops.   Never
grass and trees in their early spring foliage
looked so vividly green, while above the sky
was clear and blue as if I had left London
leagues behind.   As I advanced farther into
this wooded space the dull sounds of traffic became fainter, while ahead the continuous noise of
many cawing rooks grew louder and louder.   I
was soon under the rookery listening to and
watching the birds as they wrangled with one
another, and passed in and out among the trees
or soared above their tops.   How intensely black
they looked amidst the fresh brilliant green of
the sunlit foliage !   What wonderfully tall trees
were these where the rookery was placed !   It
was like a wood where the trees were self-
planted, and grew close together in charming
disorder, reaching a height of about one hundred
feet or more.   Of the fine sights of London so

far known to me, including the turbid, rushing
Thames, spanned by its vast stone bridges, the
cathedral with its sombre cloud-like dome, and
the endless hurrying procession of Cheapside,
this impressed me the most. The existence of
so noble a transcript of wild nature as this tall
wood with its noisy black people, so near the
heart of the metropolis, surrounded on all sides
by miles of brick and mortar and innumerable
smoking chimneys, filled me with astonishment ;
and I may say that I have seldom looked on a
scene that stamped itself on my memory in more
vivid and lasting colours. Recalling the sensations of delight I experienced then, I can now
feel nothing but horror at the thought of the
unspeakable barbarity the park authorities were
guilty of in destroying this noble grove. *Why*
was it destroyed ? It was surely worth more to
us than many of our possessions—many painted
canvases, statues, and monuments, which have
cost millions of the public money ! Of brick
and stone buildings, plain and ornamental, we
have enough to afford shelter to our bodies, and
for all other purposes, but trees of one or two
centuries' growth, the great trees that give
shelter and refreshment to the soul, are not

many in London. There must, then, have been
some urgent reason and necessity for the removal
of this temple not builded by man. It could
not surely have been for the sake of the paltry
sum which the wood was worth—paltry, that is
to say, if we compare the amount the timber-
merchant would pay for seven hundred elm-
trees with the sum of seventy-five thousand
pounds the Government gave, a little later, for
half a dozen dreary canvases from Blenheim
—dust and ashes for the hungry and thirsty!
Those who witnessed the felling of these seven
hundred trees, the tallest in London, could but
believe that the authorities had good cause for
what they did, that they had been advised by
experts in forestry; and it was vaguely thought
that the trees, which looked outwardly in so
flourishing a condition, were inwardly eaten up
with canker, and would eventually (and very
soon perhaps) have to come down. If the trees
had in very truth been dying, the authorities
would not have been justified in their action.
In the condition in which trees are placed in
London it is well nigh impossible that they
should have perfect health; but trees take long
to die, and during decay are still beautiful.

Not far from London is a tree which Aubrey
described as very old in his day, and which has
been dying since the early years of this century,
but it is not dead yet, and it may live to be
admired by thousands of pilgrims down to the
end of the twentieth century. In any case,
trees are too precious in London to be removed
because they are unsound. But the truth was,
those in Kensington Gardens were not dying
and not decayed. The very fact that they
were chosen year after year by the rooks to
build upon afforded the strongest evidence
that they were the healthiest trees in the
gardens. When they were felled a majority of
them were found to be perfectly sound. I
examined many of the finest boles, seventy and
eighty feet long, and could detect no rotten spot
in them, nor at the roots.

The only reasons I have been able to discover
as having been given for the destruction were
that grass could not be made to grow so as to
form a turf in the deep shade of the grove ; that
in wet weather, particularly during the fall of
the leaf, the ground was always sloppy and
dirty under the trees, so that no person could

walk in that part of the grounds without soiling his boots.

It will hardly be credited that the very men who did the work, before setting about it, respectfully informed the park authorities that they considered it would be a great mistake to cut the trees down, not only because they were sound and beautiful to the eye, but for other reasons. One was that the rooks would be driven away; another that this tall thick grove was a protection to the gardens, and secured the trees scattered over its northern side from the violence of the winds from the west. They were laughed at for their pains, and told that the 'screen' was not wanted, as every tree was made safe by its own roots; and as to the rooks, they would not abandon the gardens where they had bred for generations, but would build new nests on other trees. Finally, when it came to the cutting down, the men begged to be allowed to spare a few of the finest trees in the grove; and at last one tree, with no fewer than fourteen nests on it : they were sharply ordered to cut down the lot. And cut down they were, with disastrous consequences, as we know, as during the next few years many scores of the

finest trees on the north side of the gardens
were blown down by the winds, among them the
noblest tree in London—the great beech on the
east side of the wide vacant space where the
grove had stood.   The rooks, too, went away,
as they had gone before from Greenwich Park,
and as in a period of seventeen years they have
not succeeded in establishing a new rookery, we
may now regard them as lost for ever.

Seventeen years !   Some may say that this is
going too far back ; that in these fast-moving
times, crowded with historically important events,
it is hardly worth while in 1898 to recall the fact
that in 1880 a grove of seven hundred trees was
cut down in Kensington Gardens for no reason
whatever, or for a reason which would not be
taken seriously by any person in any degree
removed from the condition of imbecility !

To the nation at large the destruction of this
grove may not have been an important event,
but to the millions inhabiting the metropolis,
who in a sense form a nation in themselves, it
was exceedingly important, immeasurably more
so than most of the events recorded each year
in the ' Annual Register.'

It must be borne in mind that to a vast

majority of this population of five millions
London is a permanent home, their 'province
covered with houses' where they spend their
toiling lives far from the sights and sounds of
nature ; that the conditions being what they are,
an open space is a possession of incalculable
value, to be prized above all others, like an
amulet or a thrice-precious gem containing
mysterious health-giving properties. He, then,
who takes from London one of these sacred
possessions, or who deprives it of its value by
destroying its rural character, by cutting down
its old trees and driving out its bird life, inflicts
the greatest conceivable injury on the community, and is really a worse enemy than the
criminal who singles out an individual here and
there for attack, and who for his misdeeds is
sent to Dartmoor or to the gallows.

We give praise and glory to those who
confer lasting benefits on the community ; we
love their memories when they are no more, and
cherish their fame, and hand it on from generation to generation. In honouring them we
honour ourselves. But praise and glory would
be without significance, and love of our bene-
factors would lose its best virtue, its peculiar

sweetness, if such a feeling did not have its bitter opposite and correlative.

In conclusion of this in part mournful chapter I will relate a little experience met with in Kensington Gardens, seventeen years ago. I was in bad health at the time, with no prospect of recovery, and had been absent from London. It was a bright and beautiful morning in October, the air summer-like in its warmth, and, thinking how pleasant my favourite green and wooded haunt would look in the sunshine, I paid a visit to Kensington Gardens. Then I first saw the great destruction that had been wrought; where the grove had stood there was now a vast vacant space, many scores of felled trees lying about, and all the ground trodden and black, and variegated with innumerable yellow chips, which formed in appearance an irregular inlaid pattern.

As I stood there idly contemplating the sawn-off half of a prostrate trunk, my attention was attracted to a couple of small, ragged, shrill-voiced urchins, dancing round the wood and trying to get bits of bark and splinters off, one with a broken chopper for an implement, the

other with a small hand-hatchet, which flew off
the handle at every stroke. Seeing that I was
observing their antics, one shouted to the other,
' Say, Bill, got a penny ? '　' No, don't I wish I
had ! ' shouted the other.

' Little beggars,' thought I, ' do you really
imagine you are going to get a penny out of
me ? '　So much amused was I at their trans-
parent device that I deliberately winked an eye
—not at the urchins, but for the benefit of a
carelessly dressed, idle-looking young woman
who happened to be standing near just then,
regarding us with an expression of slight interest,
a slight smile on her rosy lips, the sunshine
resting on her beautiful sun-browned face, and
tawny bronzed hair. I must explain that I had
met her before, often and often, in London and
other towns, and in the country, and by the sea,
and on distant seas, and in many uninhabited
places, so that we were old friends and quite
familiar.

Presently an exceedingly wasted, miserable-
looking, decrepid old woman came by, bent almost
double under a ragged shawl full of sticks and
brushwood which she had gathered where the
men were now engaged in lopping off the branches

of a tree they had just felled. ' My ! she's got a
load, ain't she, Bill ? ' cried the first urchin
again. ' Oh, if we had a penny, now ! '

I asked him what he meant, and very readily
and volubly he explained that on payment of a
penny the workmen would allow any person to
take away as much of the waste wood as he
could carry, but without the penny not a chip.
I relented at that and gave them a penny, and
with a whoop of joy at their success they ran
off to where the men were working.

Then I turned to leave the gardens, nodding
a good-bye to the young woman, who was still
standing there. The slight smile and expression
of slight interest, that curious baffling expression with which she regards all our actions, from
the smallest to the greatest, came back to her
lips and face. But as she returned my glance
with her sunny eyes, behind the sunniness on
the surface there was a look of deep meaning,
such as I have occasionally seen in them before.
It seemed to be saying sorrowful and yet
comforting things to me, telling me not to grieve
overmuch at these hackings and mutilations of
the sweet places of the earth—at these losses to
be made good. It was as if she had shown me a

vision of some far time, after this London, after the dust of all her people, from park ranger to bowed-down withered old woman gathering rotten rain-sodden sticks for fuel, had been blown about by the winds of many centuries —a vision of old trees growing again on this desecrated spot as in past ages, oak and elm, and beech and chestnut, the happy, green homes of squirrel and bird and bee. It was very sweet to see London beautified and made healthy at last! And I thought, quoting Hafiz, that after a thousand years my bones would be filled with gladness, and, uprising, dance in the sepulchre.

CHAPTER VI

RECENT COLONISTS

The wood-pigeon in Kensington Gardens—Its increase—Its
beauty and charm—Perching on Shakespeare's statue in
Leicester Square—Change of habits—The moorhen—Its appearance and habits—An æsthetic bird—Its increase—The
dabchick in London—Its increase—Appearance and habits
—At Clissold Park—The stock-dove in London.

OF the species which have established colonies
in London during recent years, the wood-pigeon,
or ringdove, is the most important, being the
largest in size and the most numerous ; and it is
also remarkable on account of its beauty, melody,
and tameness. Indeed, the presence of this
bird and its abundance is a compensation for
some of our losses suffered in recent years. It
has for many of us, albeit in a less degree than
the carrion crow, somewhat of glamour, producing in such a place as Kensington Gardens
an illusion of wild nature ; and watching it
suddenly spring aloft, with loud flap of wings, to
soar circling on high and descend in a graceful

curve to its tree again, and listening to the
beautiful sound of its human-like plaint, which
may be heard not only in summer but on any
mild day in winter, one is apt to lose sight of the
increasingly artificial aspect of things; to forget
the havoc that has been wrought, until the
surviving trees—the decayed giants about whose
roots the cruel, hungry, glittering axe ever flits
and plays like a hawk-moth in the summer
twilight—no longer seem conscious of their
doom.

Twenty years ago the wood-pigeon was
almost unknown in London, the very few birds
that existed being confined to woods on the
borders of the metropolis and to some of the
old private parks—Ravenscourt, Brondesbury,
Clissold and Brockwell Parks; except two or
three pairs that bred in the group of fir trees on
the north side of Kensington Gardens, and one
pair in St. James's Park. Tree-felling caused
these birds to abandon the parks sometime
during the seventies. But from 1883, when a
single pair nested in Buckingham Palace Gardens, wood-pigeons have increased and spread
from year to year until the present time, when
there is not any park with large old trees, or

with trees of a moderate size, where these birds
are not annual breeders. As the park trees no
longer afford them sufficient accommodation
they have gone to other smaller areas, and to
many squares and gardens, private and public.
Thus, in Soho Square no fewer than six pairs
had nests last summer. It was very pleasant, a
friend told me, to look out of his window on an
April morning and see two milk-white eggs,
bright as gems in the sunlight, lying in the frail
nest in a plane tree not many yards away. In
North London these birds have increased greatly
during the last three years. Sixteen pairs bred
successfully in 1897 in Clissold Park, which is
small, and there were scores of nests in the neighbourhood, on trees growing in private grounds.

Even in the heart of the smoky, roaring City
they build their nests and rear their young on
any large tree. To other spaces, where there
are no suitable trees, they are daily visitors; and
lately I have been amused to see them come in
small flocks to the coal deposits of the Great
Western Railway at Westbourne Park. What
attraction this busy black place, vexed with
rumbling, puffing, and shrieking noises, can have
for them I cannot guess. These doves, when

disturbed, invariably fly to a terrace of houses close by and perch on the chimney-pots, a newly acquired habit.   In Leicester Square I have seen as many as a dozen to twenty birds at a time, leisurely moving about on the asphalted walks in search of crumbs of bread.   It is not unusual to see one bird perched in a pretty attitude on the head of Shakespeare's statue in the middle of the square, the most commanding position.   I never admired that marble until I saw it thus occupied by the pretty dove-coloured quest, with white collar, iridescent neck, and orange bill; since then I have thought highly of it, and am grateful to Baron Albert Grant for his gift to London, and recall with pleasure that on the occasion of its unveiling I heard its praise, as a work of art, recited in rhyme by Browning's—

> Hop-o-my-thumb, there,
> Banjo-Byron on his strum-strum, there.

I heartily wish that the birds would make use in the same way of many other statues with which our public places are furnished, if not adorned.

So numerous are the wood-pigeons at the

end of summer in their favourite parks that it is
easy for any person, by throwing a few handfuls
of grain, to attract as many as twenty or thirty
of them to his feet.   Their tameness is wonderful,
and they are delightful to look at, although so
stout of figure.   Considering their enormous
appetites, their portliness seems only natural.
But a full habit does not detract from their
beauty ; they remind us of some of our dearest
lady friends, who in spite of their two score or
more summers, and largeness where the maiden
is slim, have somehow retained loveliness and
grace.   We have seen that the London wood-
pigeon, like the London crow, occasionally
alights on buildings.   One bird comes to a ledge
of a house-front opposite my window, and walks
up and down there.   We may expect that
other changes in the birds' habits will come
about in time, if the present rate of increase
should continue.   Thus, last summer, one pair
built a nest on St. Martin's Church, Trafalgar
Square ; another pair on a mansion in Victoria
Street, Westminster.

Something further will be said of this species
in a chapter on the movements of birds in
London.

Next to the ringdove in importance—and a bird of a more fascinating personality, if such a word be admissible—is the moorhen, pretty and quaint in its silky olive-brown and slaty-grey dress, with oblique white bar on its side, and white undertail, yellow and scarlet beak and frontal shield, and large green legs. *Green-legged little hen* is its scientific name. Its motions, too, are pretty and quaint. Not without a smile can we see it going about on the smooth turf with an air of dignity incongruous in so small a bird, lifting up and setting down its feet with all the deliberation of a crane or bustard. A hundred curious facts have been recorded of this familiar species—the 'moat-hen' of old troubled days when the fighting man, instead of the schoolmaster as now, was abroad in England, and manor-houses were surrounded by moats, in which the moorhen lived, close to human beings, in a semi-domestic state. But after all that has been written, we no sooner have him near us, under our eyes, as in London to-day, than we note some new trait or pretty trick. Thus, in a pond in West London I saw a moorhen act in a manner which, so far as I know, had never been described ; and I must confess that if some

friend had related such a thing to me I should
have been disposed to think that his sight had
deceived him. This moorhen was quietly feeding
on the margin, but became greatly excited on
the appearance, a little distance away, of a second
bird. Lowering its head, it made a little rush
at, or towards, the new comer, then stopped and
went quietly back ; then made a second little
charge, and again walked back. Finally it
began to walk *backwards*, with slow, measured
steps, towards the other bird, displaying, as it
advanced, or retrograded, its open white tail, at
the same time glancing over its shoulder as if to
observe the effect on its neighbour of this new
mode of motion. Whether this demonstration
meant anger, or love, or mere fun, I cannot say.

Instances of what Ruskin has called the
moorhen's ' human domesticity of temper, with
curious fineness of sagacity and sympathies in
taste,' have been given by Bishop Stanley in his
book on birds. He relates that the young,
when able to fly, sometimes assist in rearing the
later broods, and even help the old birds to
make new nests. Of the bird's æsthetic taste
he has the following anecdote. A pair of very
tame moorhens that lived in the grounds of a

clergyman, in Cheadle, Staffordshire, in constantly adding to the materials of their nest and decorating it, made real havoc in the garden; the hen was once seen sitting on her eggs 'surrounded with a brilliant wreath of scarlet anemones.' An instance equally remarkable occurred in 1896 in Battersea Park. A pair of moorhens took it into their fantastic little heads to build their nest against a piece of wire-netting stretched across the lake at one point. It was an enormous structure, built up from the water to the top of the netting, nearly three feet high, and presented a strange appearance from the shore. On a close view the superintendent found that four tail-feathers of the peacock had been woven into its fabric, and so arranged that the four broad tips stood free above the nest, shading the cavity and sitting bird, like four great gorgeously coloured leaves.

The moorhen, like the ringdove, was almost unknown in London twenty years ago, and is now as widely diffused, but owing to its structure and habits it cannot keep pace with the other bird's increase. It must have water, and some rushes, or weeds, or bushes to make its nest in ; and wherever these are found, however small the pond may be, there the moorhen will live very contentedly.

A very few years ago it would have been a wild thing to say that the little grebe was a suitable bird for London, and if some wise ornithologist had prophesied its advent how we should all have laughed at him! For how should this timid feeble-winged wanderer be able to come and go, finding its way to and from its chosen park, in this large province covered with houses, by night, through the network of treacherous telegraph wires, in a lurid atmosphere, frightened by strange noises and confused by the glare of innumerable lamps? Of birds that get their living from the water, it would have seemed safer to look for the coming (as colonists) of the common sandpiper, kingfisher, coot, widgeon, teal : all these, also the heron and cormorant, are occasional visitors to inner London, and it is to be hoped that some of them will in time become permanent additions to the wild bird life of the metropolis.

The little grebe, before it formed a settlement, was also an occasional visitor during its spring

and autumn travels ; and in 1870, when there
was a visitation on a large scale, as many as one
hundred little grebes were seen at one time on
the Round Pond in Kensington Gardens.   But
it was not until long afterwards, about fifteen
years ago, that the first pair had the boldness
to stay and breed in one of the park lakes,
in sight of many people coming and going
every day and all day long.   This was at St.
James's Park, and from this centre the bird
has extended his range from year to year to
other parks and spaces, and is now as well
established as the ringdove and moorhen.   But,
unlike the others, he is a summer visitor, coming
in March and April, and going, no man knows
whither, in October and November.   If he were
to remain, a long severe frost might prove fatal
to the whole colony.   He lives on little fishes
and water insects, and must have open water
to fish in.

He is not a showy bird, nor large, being less
than the teal in size, and indeed is known to
comparatively few persons.   Nevertheless he is
a welcome addition to our wild bird life, and
is, to those who know him, a wonderfully
interesting little creature, clothed in a dense

unwettable plumage, olive, black, and chestnut in colour, his legs set far back—' becoming almost a fish's tail indeed, rather than a bird's

DABCHICK ON NEST

legs,' the lobed feet in shape like a horse-chestnut leaf. His habits are as curious as his structure. His nest is a raft made of a mass of water-weeds, moored to the rushes or to a drooping branch, and sometimes it breaks from its moorings and floats away, carrying eggs and sitting bird on it. On quitting the nest the bird invariably draws a coverlet of wet weeds over the eggs; the nest in appearance is then nothing but a bunch of dead vegetable rubbish floating in the water. When the young are out of the eggs, the parent birds are accustomed to take them under their wings, just as a man might take a parcel under his arm, and dive into the water.

Another curious habit of the dabchick was discovered during the summer of 1896 in Clissold Park, when, for the second time, a pair of these birds settled in the too small piece of water at that place. Unfortunately, their nest was attacked and repeatedly destroyed by the moorhens, who took a dislike to these 'new chums,' and by the swans, who probably found that the wet materials used by the little grebe in building its nest were good to eat. Now, it was observed that when the nest was made on deep water, where the swans could swim up to it, the dabchicks defended it by diving and pecking at, or biting, the webbed feet of the assailants under water. It was a curious duel between a pigmy and a giant—one a stately man-of-war floating on the water, the other a small submerged torpedo, very active and intelligent. The swans were greatly disconcerted and repeatedly driven off by means of this strategy, but in the end the brave little divers were beaten, and reared no young.

The moral of this incident, which applies not only to Clissold but to Brockwell, Dulwich, and to a dozen other parks, is that you cannot have a big aquatic happy family in a very small pond.

But it is extremely encouraging to all those who wish for a 'better friendship' with the fowls of the air to find that this contest was watched with keen interest and sympathy with the defenders by the superintendent of a London park and the park constables.

It is curious to note that the three species we have been considering, differing so widely in their structures and habits, should be so closely associated in the history of London wild bird life. That they should have established colonies at very nearly about the same time, and very nearly at the same centre, from which they have subsequently spread over the metropolis; and that this centre, the cradle of the London races of these birds, should continue to be their most favoured resort. Seeing the numbers of wood-pigeons to-day, and their tameness everywhere, the statement will seem

almost incredible to many readers that only
fifteen years ago, one spring morning, the head
gardener at Buckingham Palace, full of excitement, made a hurried visit to a friend to tell
him that a pair of these birds had actually built
a nest on a tree in the Palace grounds.   Up
till now the birds are most numerous in this
part of London.   The moorhen, I believe, bred
first at St. James's Park about seventeen years
ago ; a few days ago—January 1898—I saw
twelve of these birds in a little scattered flock
feeding in the grass in this park.   In no other
public park in London can so many be seen
together.   The dabchick first bred in St. James's
Park about fifteen years ago, and last summer,
1897, as many as seven broods were brought
out.   In no other London park were there
more than two broods.

The three species described are the only permanent additions in recent years to the wild bird
life of the metropolis.   But when it is considered
that their colonies were self-planted, and have
shown a continuous growth, while great changes
of decrease and increase have meanwhile been
going on in the old-established colonies, we find

good reason for the hope that other species, previously unknown to the metropolis, will be added from time to time. We know that birds attract birds, both their own and other kinds. Even now there may be some new-comers— pioneers and founders of fresh colonies—whose presence is unsuspected, or known only to a very few observers. I have been informed by Mr. Howard Saunders that he has seen the stock-dove in one of the West-end parks, and that a friend of his had independently made the discovery that this species is now a visitor to, and possibly a resident in, London. One would imagine the stock-dove to be a species well suited to thrive with us, as it would find numberless breeding-holes both in the decayed trees in the parks and in big buildings, in which to rear its young in safety. I should prefer to see the turtle-dove, a much prettier and more graceful bird, with a better voice, but beggars must not be choosers ; with the stock-dove established, London will possess three of the four doves indigenous in these islands, and the turtle-dove—at present an annual breeder in woods quite near to London—may follow by-and-by to complete the quartette.

CHAPTER VII

LONDON'S LITTLE BIRDS

Number of species, common and uncommon—The London sparrow—His predominance, hardiness, and intelligence—A pet sparrow—Breeding irregularities—A love-sick bird—Sparrow shindies: their probable cause—' Sparrow chapels '—Evening in the parks—The starling—His independence —Characteristics—Blackbird, thrush, and robin—White blackbirds—The robin—Decrease in London—Habits and disposition.

THERE are not more than about twenty species of small passerine birds that live all the year in London proper. The larger wild birds that breed in London within the five-mile radius are eight species, or if we add the semi-domestic pigeon or rock-dove, there are nine. Of the twenty small birds, it is surprising to find that only five can be described as really common, including the robin, which in recent years has ceased to be abundant in the interior parks, and has quite disappeared from the squares, burial grounds, and other small open spaces. The five familiar species are the sparrow, starling, black-

bird, song-thrush or throstle, and robin, and in
the present chapter these only will be dealt with.
All the other resident species found in London
proper, or inner London—missel-thrush, wren,
hedge-sparrow, nuthatch, tree-creeper, tits of
five species, chaffinch, bullfinch, greenfinch, and
yellowhammer, also the summer visitants, and
some rare residents occasionally to be found
breeding on the outskirts of the metropolis—will
be spoken of in subsequent chapters descriptive
of the parks and open spaces.

Here once more the sparrow takes pre-
cedence. ' What! the sparrow again ! ' the
reader may exclaim; 'I thought we had quite
finished with that little bird, and were now
going on to something else.' Unfortunately, as
we have seen, there is little else to go on to
until we get to the suburbs, and that little bird
the sparrow is not easily finished with.   Besides,
common as he is, intimately known to every
man, woman, and child in the metropolis, even
to the meanest gutter child in the poorest
districts, it is always possible to find something
fresh to say of a bird of so versatile a mind, so
highly developed, so predominant.   He must
indeed be gifted with remarkable qualities to

have risen to such a position, to have occupied, nay conquered, London, and made its human inhabitants food-providers to his nation; and, finally, to have kept his possession so long without any decay of his pristine vigour, despite the unhealthy conditions. He does not receive, nor does he need, that fresh blood from the country which we poor human creatures must have, or else perish in the course of a very few generations. Nor does he require change of air. It is commonly said that ' town sparrows' migrate to the fields in summer, to feast on corn ' in the milk,' and this is true of our birds in the outlying suburbs, who live in sight of the fields; farther in, the sparrow never leaves his London home. I know that *my* sparrows—a few dozen that breed and live under my eyes— never see the country, nor any park, square, or other open space.

The hardiness and adaptiveness of the bird must both be great to enable it to keep its health and strength through the gloom and darkness of London winters. There is no doubt that many of our caged birds would perish at this season if they did not feed by gas or candle light. When they do not so feed it is found that the mortality, presumably from starvation, is very considerable. During December and January the London night is nearly seventeen hours in length, as it is sooner dark and later light than in the country ; while in cold and foggy weather the birds feed little or not at all. They keep in their roosting-holes, and yet they do not appear to suffer. After a spell of frosty and very dark weather I have counted the sparrows I am accustomed to observe, and found none missing.

But the sparrow's chief advantage over other species doubtless lies in his greater intelligence. That ineradicable suspicion with which he regards the entire human race, and which one is sometimes inclined to set down to sheer stupidity, is, in the circumstances he exists in, his best policy. He has good cause to doubt the friendliness of his human neighbours, and his principle is, not to run risks ; when in doubt, keep away. Thus, when the roads are swept the sparrows will go to the dirt and rubbish heaps, and search in them for food ; then they will fly up to any window-sill and eat the bread they find put there for them. But let them see any rubbish of any description there, anything but bread—a bit of string, a chip of wood, a scrap of paper, white or blue or yellow, or a rag, or even a penny piece, and at the first sight of it away they will dart, and not return until the dangerous object has been removed. A pigeon or starling would come and take the food without paying any attention to the strange object which so startled the sparrow. They are less cunning. Without doubt there are many boys and men in all parts of London who amuse themselves by trying to take sparrows, and the result of their attempts is that the birds decline to trust anyone.

In this extreme suspiciousness, and in their habits generally, all sparrows appear pretty much alike to us. When we come to know them intimately, in the domestic state, we find that there is as much individual character in sparrows as in other highly intelligent creatures. The most interesting tame sparrow I have known in London was the pet of a lady of my acquaintance. This bird, however, was not a cockney sparrow from the nest : he was hatched on the other side of the Channel, and his owner rescued him, when young and scarce able to fly, from some street urchins in a suburb of Paris, who were playing with and tormenting him. In his

London home he grew up to be a handsome
bird, brighter in plumage than our cock
sparrows usually seem, even in the West-end
parks. He was strongly attached to his mistress,
and liked to play with and to be caressed by
her; when she sat at work he would perch contentedly by her side by the half-hour chirruping
his sparrow-music, interspersed with a few notes
borrowed from caged songsters. He displayed a
marked interest in her dress and ornaments, and
appeared to take pleasure in richly coloured
silks and satins, and in gold and precious stones.
But all these things did not please him in the
same degree, and the sight of some ornaments
actually angered him : he would scold and peck
at the brooch or necklace, or whatever it was,
which he did not like, and if no notice was
taken at first, he would work himself into a
violent rage, and the offensive jewel would have
to be taken off and put out of sight. He also
had his likes and dislikes among the inmates
and guests in the house. He would allow me
to sit by him for an hour, taking no notice, but
if I made any advance he would ruffle up his
plumage, and tell me in his unmistakable
sparrow-language to keep my distance. Once

he took a sudden violent hatred to his owner's
maid ; no sooner would she enter the room
where the sparrow happened to be than he
would dart at her face and peck and beat her
with his wings ; and as he could not be made to
like, nor even to tolerate her, she had to be
discharged. It was, however, rare for him to
abuse his position of first favourite so grossly as
on this occasion. He was on the whole a good-
tempered bird, and had a happy life, spending
the winter months each year in Italy, where his
mistress had a country house, and returning in
the spring to London. Then, very unexpectedly,
his long life of eighteen years came to an end ;
for up to the time of dying he showed no sign
of decadence. To the last his plumage and disposition were bright, and his affection for his
mistress and love for his own music un-
abated.

After all, it must be said that the sparrow,
as a pet, has his limitations ; he is not, mentally,
as high as the crow, aptly described by Mac-
gillivray as the ' great sub-rational chief of the
kingdom of birds.' And however luxurious the
home we may give him, he is undoubtedly
happier living his own independent life, a

married bird, making slovenly straw nests under the tiles, and seeking his food in the gutter.

Many years ago Dr. Gordon Stables said, in an article on the sparrow, that he felt convinced from his own observation of these birds that curious irregularities in their domestic or matrimonial relations were of very frequent occurrence, a fact which the ornithologists had overlooked. Last summer I had proof that such irregularities do occur, but I very much doubt that they are so common as he appears to believe.

I had one pair of sparrows breeding in a hole under the eaves at the top of the house, quite close to a turret window, from which I look down upon and observe the birds, and on the sill of which I place bread for them. This pair reared brood after brood, from April to November, and so long as they found bread on the window-sill they appeared to feed their young almost exclusively on it, although it is not their natural food ; but there was no green place near where caterpillars might be found, and I dare say the young sparrow has an adaptive stomach. At all events broods of four and five were successively brought out and taught to feed on

the window-sill.   After a few days' holiday the
old birds would begin to tidy up the nest to
receive a fresh clutch of eggs.   In July I noticed
that a second female, the wife, as it appeared, of
a neighbouring bird, had joined the first pair,
and shared in the tasks of incubation and of
feeding the young.   The cast-off cock-sparrow
had followed her to her new home, and was
constantly hanging about the nest trying to
coax his wife to go back to him.   Day after day,
and all day long, he would be there, and sitting
on the slates quite close to the nest he would
begin his chirrup — chirrup — chirrup ; and
gradually as time went on, and there was no
response, he would grow more and more excited,
and throw his head from side to side, and rock
his body until he would be lying first on one
side, then the other, and after a while he would
make a few little hops forward, trailing his
wings and tail on the slates, then cast himself
down once more.   Something in his monotonous
song with its not unmusical rhythm, and his
extravagant love-sick imploring gestures and
movements, reminded me irresistibly of Chevalier
in the character of Mr. 'Enry 'Awkins—his whole
action on the stage, the thin piping cockney

voice, the trivial catching melody, and, I had
almost added, the very words—

> So 'elp me bob, I'm crazy !
> Lizer, you're a daisy !
> Won't yer share my 'umble 'ome ?
> Oh, Lizer ! sweet Lizer !

And so on, and on, until one of the birds in the
nest would come out and furiously chase him
away.   Then he would sit on some chimney-
pipe twenty or thirty yards off, silent and solitary ;
but by-and-by, seeing the coast clear, he would
return and begin his passionate pleading once
more.

This went on until the young birds were
brought out, after which they all went away for
a few days, and then the original pair returned.
No doubt 'Enry 'Awkins had got his undutiful
doner back.

The individual sparrow is, however, little
known to us : we regard him rather as a species,
or race, and he interests the mass of people
chiefly in his social character when he is seen in
companies, and crowds, and multitudes.   He is
noisiest and attracts most attention when there
is what may be called a ' shindy ' in the sparrow

community. Shindies are of frequent occurrence
all the year round, and may arise from a variety
of causes ; my belief is that, as they commonly
take place at or near some favourite nesting or
roosting site, they result from the sparrow's sense
of proprietorship and his too rough resentment
of any intrusion into his own domain. Sparrows
in London mostly remain paired all the year,
and during the winter months roost in the
breeding-hole, often in company with the young
of the last-raised brood. Why all the neighbours
rush in to take part in the fight is not so easy to
guess : possibly they come in as would-be peace-
makers, or policemen, but are themselves so
wildly excited that they do nothing except to
get into each other's way and increase the
confusion.

Of more interest are those daily gatherings
of a pacific nature at some favourite meeting-
place, known to Londoners as a ' sparrows'
chapel.' A large tree, or group of trees, in
some garden, square, or other space, is used by
the birds, and here they are accustomed to
congregate at various times, when the rain is
over, or when a burst of sunshine after gloomy
weather makes them glad, and at sunset. Their

chorus of ringing chirruping sounds has an
exceedingly pleasant effect ; for although compared with the warblers' singing it may be a
somewhat rude music, by contrast with the noise
of traffic and raucous cries from human throats
it is very bright and glad and even beautiful,
voicing a wild, happy life.

It is interesting and curious to find that this
habit of concert-singing at sunset, although not
universal, is common among passerine birds in
all regions of the globe. And when a bird has
this habit he will not omit his vesper song, even
when the sun is not visible and when rain is
falling. In some mysterious way he knows that
the great globe is sinking beneath the horizon.
Day is over, he can feed no more until
to-morrow, in a few minutes he will be sleeping
among the clustering leaves, but he must sing
his last song, must join in that last outburst of
melody to express his overflowing joy in life.

This is a habit of our sparrow, and even on
the darkest days, when days are shortest, any
person desirous of hearing the birds need only
consult the almanac to find out the exact time
of sunset, then repair to a ' chapel,' and he will
not be disappointed.

In some of the parks, notably at Battersea, where the birds are in thousands, the effect of so many voices all chirruping together is quite wonderful, and very delightful.

The time will come, let us hope, when for half a dozen species of small birds in London we shall have two dozen, or even fifty; until then the sparrow, even the common gutter-sparrow, is a bird to be thankful for.

The starling ranks second to the sparrow in numbers; but albeit second, the interval is very great: the starlings' thousands are but a small tribe compared to the sparrows' numerous nation.

It has been said that the starling is almost as closely associated with man as the sparrow. That is hardly the case; in big towns the sparrow, like the rat and black beetle, although not in so unpleasant a way, is parasitical on man, whereas the starling is perfectly independent. He frequents human habitations because they provide him with suitable breeding-holes; he builds in a house, or barn, or church tower, just as he does in a hole in a tree in a wild forest, or a hole in the rock on some sea-cliff,

where instead of men and women he has puffins,
guillemots, and gannets for neighbours. The
roar of the sea or the jarring noises of human
traffic and industry—it is all one to the starling.
That is why he is a London bird. In the
breeding season he is to be found diffused over
the entire metropolis, an astonishing fact when
we consider that he does not, like the sparrow,
find his food in the roads, back gardens, and
small spaces near his nest, but, like the rook,
must go a considerable distance for it.

Two seasons ago (1896) one pair of starlings
had their nest close to my house—a treeless
district, most desolate. When the young were
hatched I watched the old birds going and
coming, and on leaving the nest they invariably
flew at a good height above the chimney-pots
and telegraph wires, in the direction of the
Victoria Gate of Hyde Park. They returned
the same way. It is fully two miles to the park
in that direction. The average number of eggs
in a starling's nest is six; and assuming that
these birds had four or five young, we can
imagine what an enormous labour it must have
been to supply them with suitable insect food,
each little beakful of grubs involving a return

journey of at least four miles ; and the grubs
would certainly be very much more difficult to
find on the trodden sward of Hyde Park than
in a country meadow.   I pitied these brave
birds every day, when I watched them from my
turret window, going and coming, and at the
same time I rejoiced to think that this pair, and
hundreds of other pairs with nests just as far
from their scanty feeding-grounds, were yet
able to rear their young each season in London.

For the starling is really a splendid bird as
birds are with us in this distant northern land—
splendid in his spangled glossy dress of metallic
purple, green, and bronze, a singer it is always
pleasant to listen to, a flyer in armies and
crowds whose aërial evolutions in autumn and
winter, before settling to roost each evening,
have long been the wonder and admiration of
mankind.   He inhabits London all the year
round, but not in the same numbers : in the
next chapter more will be said on this point.
He also sings throughout the year ; on any
autumn or winter day a small company or flock
of a dozen or two of birds may be found in any
park containing large trees, and it is a delight
that never grows stale to listen to the musical

conversation, or concert of curiously contrasted
sounds, perpetually going on among them. The
airy whistle, the various chirp, the clink-clink

LONDON STARLINGS

as of a cracked bell, the low chatter of mixed
harsh and musical sounds, the kissing and
finger-cracking, and those long metallic notes,
as of a saw being filed not unmusically, or (as a
friend suggests) as of milking a cow in a tin
pail ;—however familiar you may be with the

starling, you cannot listen to one of their choirs
without hearing some new sound. There is
more variety in the starling than in any other
species, and not only in his language; if you observe him closely for a short time, he will treat
you to a sudden and surprising transformation.
Watch him when absorbed in his own music,
especially when emitting his favourite saw-filing
or milking-a-cow-in-a-tin-pail sounds : he trembles
on his perch—shivers as with cold—his feathers
puffed out, his wings hanging as if broken, his
beak wide open, and the long pointed feathers
of his swollen throat projected like a ragged
beard. He is then a most forlorn-looking object,
apparently broken up and falling to pieces ;
suddenly the sounds cease, and in the twinkling
of an eye he is once more transformed into the
neat, compact, glossy, alert starling !

Something further may be said about the pair
of starlings that elected to breed the summer
before last in sight of my top windows, in that
brick desert where my home is. When they
brought out and led their young away, I
wondered if they would ever return to such a
spot. Surely, thought I, they will have some
recollection of the vast labour of rearing a

nestful of young at such a distance from their feeding-ground, and when summer comes once more will be tempted to settle somewhere nearer to the park. The Albert Memorial, for instance, gorgeous with gold and bright colour, might attract them; certainly there was room for them, since it had in the summer of 1896 but one pair of starlings for tenants. It was consequently something of a surprise when, on March 23 last spring, early in the morning, the birds reappeared at the same place, and spent over an hour in fluttering about and exploring the old breeding-hole, perching on the slates and chimney-pots, and clinging to the brick wall, fluttering their wings, screaming and whistling as if almost beside themselves with joy to be at home once more.

Brave and faithful starlings! we hardly deserve to have you back, since London has not been too kind to her feathered children. Quite lately she has driven out her rooks, who were faithful too; and long ago she got rid of her ravens; and to her soaring kites she meted out still worse treatment, pulling down their last nest in 1777 from the trees in Gray's Inn Gardens, and cutting open the young birds to find out, in the interests of ornithological science, what they had eaten !

Between the starling and the next in order, the blackbird, there is again a very great difference with regard to numbers. The former counts thousands, the latter hundreds. Between blackbird and song-thrush, or throstle, there is not a wide difference, but if we take the whole of London, the blackbird is much more numerous. After these two, at a considerable distance, comes the robin. In suburban grounds and gardens these three common species are equally abundant. But in these same private places, which ring the metropolis round with innumerable small green refuges, or sanctuaries, several other species which are dying out in the parks and open spaces of inner London are also common—wren, hedge-sparrow, blue, cole, and great tits, chaffinch, and greenfinch—and of these no more need be said in this chapter.

As we have seen, there is always a great interest shown (by the collector especially) in that not very rare phenomenon, an abnormally white bird. But in London the bird-killers are restrained, and the white specimen is sometimes able to keep his life for a few or even for several months. Recently (1897) a very beautiful white blackbird was to be seen in Kensington Gardens, in the Flower Walk, east of the Albert Memorial. He was the successor to a wholly milk-white blackbird that lived during the summer of 1895 in the shrubberies of Kensington Palace, and was killed by some scoundrel, who no doubt hoped to sell its carcass to some bird-stuffer. Its crushed body was found by one of the keepers in a thick holly-bush close to the public path ; the slayer had not had time to get into the enclosure to secure his prize.

The other bird had some black and deep brown spots on his mantle, and a few inky black tail and wing feathers—a beautiful Dominican dress. But when I first saw him, rushing out of a black holly-bush, one grey misty morning in October, his exceeding whiteness startled me, and I was ready to believe that I had beheld a blackbird's ghost, when the bird, startled too, emitted his prolonged chuckle, proving him to be no supernatural thing, but only a fascinating freak of nature. He lived on, very much

admired, until the end of March last year (1897),
having meanwhile found a mate, and was then
killed by a cat.

The robin, although common as ever in all
the more rural parts of London—the suburban
districts where there are gardens with shrubs
and trees—is now growing sadly scarce everywhere in the interior of the metropolis. In
1865 the late Shirley Hibberd wrote that this
bird was very common in London: 'Robins
are seen among the hay-carts at Whitechapel,
Smithfield, and Cumberland Markets, in all the
squares, in Lincoln's Inn, Gray's Inn, and
other gardens, in the open roadway of Farring-
don Street, Ludgate Hill, the Strand, and
Blackfriars Road; nay, I once saw a robin on
a lovely autumn afternoon perch upon the
edge of a gravestone in St. Paul's Churchyard
and trill out a carol as sweetly as in any rural
nook at home.'

Now the robin has long vanished from all
these public places, even from the squares that
are green, and that he is becoming very scarce
in all the interior parks I shall have occasion to
show in later chapters. It is a great pity that

this should be so, as this bright little bird is a universal favourite on account of his confidence in and familiarity with man, and his rare beauty, and because, as becomes a cousin of the nightingale, he is a very sweet singer. Moreover, just as his red breast shines brightest in autumn and winter, when all things look grey and desolate, or white with the snow's universal whiteness, so does his song have a peculiar charm and almost unearthly sweetness in the silent songless season. It is not strange that in credulous times man's imagination should have endowed so loved a bird with impossible virtues, that it should have been believed that he alone—heaven's little feathered darling—cared for ' the friendless bodies of unburied men ' and covered them with leaves, and was not without some supernatural faculties. Nor can it be said that all these pretty fables have quite faded out of the rustic mind. But, superstition apart, the robin is still a first favourite and dear to everyone, and some would gladly think he is a *better* bird, in the sense of being gentler, sweeter-tempered, more affectionate and *human*, than other feathered creatures. But it is not so, the tender expression of his large dark eye is deceptive. The late Mr.

Tristram-Valentine, writing of the starling in
London, its neat, bright, glossy appearance, compared with that of the soot-blackened disreput-
able-looking sparrow, says ' the starling always
looks like a gentleman.' In like manner the
robin will always be a robin, and act like one,
in London or out of it—the most unsocial,
fierce-tempered little duellist in the feathered
world. Now I wish to point out that this
fierce intolerant spirit of our bird is an advantage in London, if we love robins and are
anxious to have plenty of them.

It is a familiar fact that at the end of
summer the adult robins disappear ; that they
remain in hiding in the shade of the evergreens
and thick bushes until they have got a new
dress, and have recovered their old vigour ; that
when they return to the world, so to speak,
and find their young in possession of their
home and territory, they set themselves to re-
conquer it. For the robin will not tolerate
another robin in that portion of a garden,
shrubbery, orchard, or plantation which he
regards as his very own. A great deal of
fighting then takes place between old and young
birds, and these fights in many instances end

fatally to one of the combatants. The raven
has the same savage disposition and habit with
regard to its young; and when a young raven,
in disposition a 'chip of the old block,' refuses
to go when ordered, and fights to stay, it
occasionally happens that one of the birds gets
killed. But the raven has a tremendous
weapon, a stone axe, in his massive beak; how
much greater the fury and bulldog tenacity of
the robin must be to kill one of his own kind
with so feeble a weapon as his small soft bill!
At the end of the summer of 1896 two robins
were observed fighting all day long in the
private gardens of Kensington Palace, the fight
ending in the death of one of the birds.

Finally, as a result of all the chasing and
fighting that goes on, the young birds are
driven out to find homes for themselves. In
London, in the interior parks, not many young
robins are reared, but many of those that
have been reared in the suburban districts drift
into London, and altogether a considerable
number of birds roam about the metropolis in
search of some suitable green spot to settle in;
and I will only add here, in anticipation of what
will be said in a later chapter, that if suitable

places were provided for them, the robins would increase year by year from this natural cause.

There are other movements of robins in London which it will be more in order to notice in the next chapter.

CHAPTER VIII

MOVEMENTS OF LONDON BIRDS

Migration as seen in London—Swallows in the parks—Fieldfares—A flock of wild geese—Autumn movements of resident
species—Wood-pigeons—A curious habit—Dabchicks and
moorhens—Crows and rooks—The Palace daws—Starlings
—Robins—A Tower robin and the Tower sparrows—Passage
birds in the parks—Small birds wintering in London—
Influx of birds during severe frosts—Occasional visitors—
The black-headed gull—A winter scene in St. James's Park.

THE seasonal movements of the strict migrants
are little noticed in London ; there are few such
species that visit, fewer still that remain any
time with us. And when they come we scarcely
see them : they are not like the residents,
reacted on and modified by their surroundings,
made tame, ready to feed from our hands, to
thrust themselves at all times upon our attention.
Nevertheless we do occasionally see something
of these shyer wilder ones, the strangers and
passengers ; and in London, as in the rural
districts, it is the autumnal not the vernal

migration which impresses the mind.   Birds are
seldom seen arriving in spring.   Walking to-day
in some park or garden, we hear the first willow-
wren's delicate tender warble among the fresh
April foliage.   It was not heard yesterday, but
the small modest-coloured singer may have been
there nevertheless, hidden and silent among the
evergreens.   The birds that appear in the
autumn are plainly travellers that have come
from some distant place, and have yet far to go.
Wheatears may be seen if looked for in August
on Hampstead Heath, and occasionally a few
other large open spaces in or near London.   In
September and October swallows and martins
put in an appearance, and although they refuse
to make their summer home in inner London,
they often come in considerable numbers and
remain for many days, even for weeks, in the
parks in autumn.

It has been conjectured that the paucity of
winged insect life in London is the cause of the
departure of swallows and house-martins as
breeding species.   Yet in the autumn of 1896,
from September to the middle of October,
hundreds of these birds lived in the central and
many other parks in London, and doubtless they

found a sufficiency of food in spite of the cold east winds which prevailed at that time.

FIELDFARES AT THE TOWER

Among the winter visitors to the outskirts of the metropolis, the fieldfare is the most abundant as well as the most attractive. During the winters of 1895–6 and 1896–7 I saw them on numberless occasions at Wimbledon, Richmond, Hampstead Heath, Bostall Woods, Hackney Marsh, Wanstead, Dulwich, Brockwell Park, Streatham, and other open spaces and woods round London. In the gardens of the outer suburbs there is always a great profusion of winter berries, and the felts seen in these places are probably regular visitors. Certainly they are tamer than fieldfares are apt to be in the country, but they seldom penetrate far into the brick-and-mortar wilderness. I have seen a few in Kensington Gardens, and in November, 1896, a few fieldfares alighted on a tree at the Tower of London. Stranger still, in February 1897 a flock of wild geese was observed flying over the Tower : the birds went down the river flying low, as it was noticed that when they passed over the Tower Bridge they were not higher than the pinnacles of the two big towers.

The birds that are strange to London eyes are very nearly all seen in the autumn, from September to November. At this mutable season a person who elects to spend his nights on the roof, with rugs and an umbrella to keep out

LOVE-SICK COCK SPARROW

FEEDING THE GULLS IN ST. JAMES'S PARK

cold and wet, may be rewarded by hearing far-off shrill delicate noises of straggling sandpipers or other shore birds on passage, or the mysterious cry of the lapwing, ' wailing his way from cloud to cloud.'

All these rare sights and sounds are for the very patient watchers and listeners ; nevertheless they are the only ' authentic tidings ' the Londoner receives of that great and wonderful wave of life which travels southward over half the globe in advance of winter. This annual exodus and sublime flight to distant delectable regions beyond the sea is, however, only taken part in by some of the feathered people ; meanwhile the others that remain to brave the cold and scarcity are also seen to be infected with a restless spirit and desire of change. The starling, missel-thrush, larks and pipits, and other kinds, alter their way of life, uniting in flocks and becoming wanderers over the face of the country. Finches, too, go a-gypsying : the more sedentary species leave their breeding-haunts for suitable winter quarters ; and everywhere there is a great movement, a changing of places, packing and scattering, a hurrying to and fro all over the land.

The London birds are no exception, although their autumnal movements have hitherto attracted little attention. These movements are becoming more noticeable, owing to changes going on in the character of the metropolitan bird population. The sparrow, as we have seen, does not leave home, but recently there has been a great increase in the more vagrant species, the starling and wood-pigeon especially. During the last few years the wood-pigeon has been growing somewhat more domestic, and less inclined to leave town than formerly, but from time to time the old wandering instinct reasserts itself, and it was observed that during the autumn of 1896 a majority of the birds left London. At Lincoln's Inn Fields there were thirteen birds down to the end of September, then all but one disappeared. This solitary stayer-at-home had been sprung upon and injured by a cat some time before the day of departure.

Last year, 1897, the autumnal exodus was even greater. Thus, on October 25 I walked the whole length of the three central parks, and saw no pigeons except one pair of young birds not long out of the nest, in Hyde Park, and one parent bird feeding them. The other parent had probably gone away to the country, leaving his mate to rear this very late brood as best she could.   Doubtless many of these wanderers from the metropolis get killed in the country, but in December and January the survivors return to the safety of the parks, and to a monotonous diet of stale bread.

It is probable that with the change of temperature in September and October the London wood-pigeons, like so many birds, are seized by a restless and roving spirit ; but I am inclined to believe that the taste of wild nuts and fruits, which they get in the parks at that season, is one cause of their going away.   They do not get much of this natural food ; they first strip the oaks of their acorns almost before they are quite ripe, depriving the London urchins of their little harvest, and then attack the haws and holly-berries ; and when this small supply has been exhausted the birds go further afield in search of more.

On the evening of August 26, 1897, I saw a number of wood-pigeons feeding on the haws in a manner quite new in my experience.   There were twelve or fourteen birds on a good-sized thorn-tree growing in Buckingham Palace

WOOD-PIGEON FEEDING ON HAWS

grounds ; but the berries on this tree grew at
the tips of long slender branches and could not
have been reached by the birds in the ordinary

way. The pigeons would settle on a branch and then begin moving cautiously towards the points, the branch bending beneath the weight more and more until the bird, unable to keep any longer *on* the branch, would suddenly turn over and remain hanging head down, suspended by its clinging feet. In this position, by stretching its neck it would be able to reach the berries, which it would then leisurely devour. As many as four or five birds were seen at one time hanging in this way, appearing with wings half-open like dead or wounded birds tied by their feet to the branchlets, from which they were suspended. Since witnessing this curious scene I have been told by Mr. Coppin, the superintendent at Battersea Park, that he has seen the wood-pigeons at that place acting in the same way. It is probably a habit of the birds which has hitherto escaped notice.

The dabchicks leave London in the autumn and return in spring : they may be looked for in the ornamental waters as early as the third week in March. The moorhens formerly disappeared from London in winter ; they are now residents throughout the year in a few of the parks where there is shelter, and during severe frosts they feed at the same table with the ornamental waterfowl. From all the smaller lakes which they have recently colonised they vanish in cold weather. In autumn they wander about a good deal by night; any small piece of water will attract them, and their cries will be heard during the dark hours; before it is light they will be gone.

Crows and rooks are most often seen in London during the winter months. Many rooks have their winter roosting-place in Richmond Park, and small bands of these birds visit the central parks and other open spaces. On the morning of February 3, 1897, about fifty rooks visited Kensington Gardens and fed for some hours on the strip of grassed land adjoining the palace. The whole jackdaw colony, numbering twenty-four birds, fed with them, and when, about twelve o'clock, the visitors rose up and flew away, the daws, after seeing them off, returned in a body to the tree-tops near the palace, and for the rest of the day continued in an excited state. From time to time they would rush up with a loud clamour, then return to the tree-tops, where they would sit close together and silent as if expecting something, and at intervals of a minute or two a simultaneous cry would burst from them.

I have observed that on winter evenings these daws fly away from the gardens in a north-westerly direction : where their winter roosting-place is I have not discovered.

The starling is the most interesting London bird in his autumn movements. It is only at the end of July, when they are gathered in large bodies, that some idea can be formed of their numbers. Flocks of a dozen to forty or fifty birds may be seen in any park and green space any day throughout the winter ; these are the birds that winter with us, and are but a small remnant of the entire number that breed in London. At the end of June the starlings begin to congregate every evening at their favourite roosting-places. Of these there are several, the most favoured being the islands in the ornamental water at Regent's Park, the island in the Serpentine, and at Buckingham Palace grounds and Battersea Park. The last is the most important. Before sunset the birds are seen pouring in, flock after flock, from all quarters, until the trees on the island are black with their thousands, and the noise of their singing and chattering is so great that a person standing on the edge of the lake can hardly hear himself speak. These meeting places are evidently growing in favour, and if the autumn of 1898 shows as great an increase as those of 1896 and 1897 over previous years, London will have as compensation for its lost rookeries some very fine clouds of starlings. At the beginning of October most of the birds go away to spend the winter in the country, or possibly abroad. In February and March they begin to reappear in small flocks, and gradually scatter over the whole area of the metropolis, each pair going back to its old nesting-hole.

The annual scattering of robins at the end of summer, when, after the moult, the old birds attack and drive away the young, has been described in the last chapter. This habit of the bird alone would cause a good deal of moving about of the London robins each year, but it is also a very general belief of ornithologists that at this season there is a large migratory movement of young robins throughout the country. At all events, it is a fact that in August and September robins go about in London a good deal, and frequently appear in the most unlikely places. Some of these are no doubt birds of the year hatched in London or the suburbs, and others may be migrating robins passing through.

At the Tower of London robins occasionally appear in autumn, but soon go away. The last one that came settled down and was a great favourite with the people there for about two months, being very friendly, coming to window-sills for crumbs, and singing every day very beautifully. Then one day he was seen in the General's garden wildly dashing about, hotly pursued by seven or eight sparrows, and as he was never seen again it was conjectured that the sparrows had succeeded in killing him. The robin is a high-spirited creature, braver than most birds, and a fair fighter, but against such a gang of feathered murderous ruffians, bent on his destruction, he would stand no chance.

The Tower sparrows, it may be added, appear to be about the worst specimens of their class in London. They are always at war with the pigeons and starlings, and would gladly drive them out if they could. It is a common

thing for some foreign bird to escape from its
cage on board ship and to take refuge in the
trees and gardens of the Tower, but woe to the
escaped captive and stranger in a strange land
who seeks safety in such a place! Immediately
on his arrival the sparrows are all up against
him, not to 'heave half a brick at him,' since
they are not made that way, but to hunt him
from place to place until they have driven him,
weak with fatigue and terror, into a corner
where they can finish him with their bludgeon
beaks.

This violence towards strangers of the Tower
sparrow is not to be wondered at, since this
unpleasant disposition or habit is common to
many species. The prophet Jeremiah had
observed it when he said, 'Mine heritage is
unto me as a speckled bird, the birds round
about are against her.' To the Tower sparrows every feathered stranger is conspicuously
speckled, and they are against her. The wonder
is that they should keep up their perpetual little
teasing warfare against the pigeons and starlings,
their neighbours from time immemorial. One
would have imagined that so intelligent and
practical a bird as the sparrow, after vainly trying

for several centuries to drive out his fellow tenants, would have made peace with them and found some more profitable outlet for his superabundant energies. Possibly the introduction of a few feathered policemen—owls, or magpies, or sparrow hawks—would have the effect of making him a less quarrelsome neighbour.

In autumn and in spring a variety of summer visitants, mostly warblers, pass through London, delaying a little in its green spaces. In September we are hardly cognisant of these small strangers within our gates, all but one or two being silent at that season. In April and May, in many of the parks, we may hear the chiff-chaff, willow-wren, blackcap, sedge-warbler, the whitethroat, occasionally the cuckoo, and a few other rarer species, but they sing little, and soon leave us to seek better breeding-sites than the inner parks offer.

While some of our birds, as we have seen, forsake us at the approach of cold weather, some for a short period, others to remain away until the following spring, a small contrary movement of birds into London is going on. These winterers with us come not in battalions

and are little remarked. They are to be found,
a few here and a few there, all over London,
wherever there are trees and bushes, but less
in the public parks than in private grounds,
cemeteries, and other quiet spots. Thus, during
the last two exceptionally mild winters a few
skylarks have lived contentedly in the comparatively small green area at Lambeth Palace.
Nunhead Cemetery is a favourite winter resort
of a number of small birds—starlings, chaffinches, and greenfinches, and a few of other
species.   Chaffinches are found in winter in
several of the open spaces where they do not
breed, and among other species to be found
wintering in the quiet green spots in small
numbers are linnets, goldfinches, pipits, and the
pied wagtail.

In exceptionally severe winters birds come
into London in considerable numbers—rooks,
starlings, larks, blackbirds and thrushes, finches,
and other small species—and they then visit
not only the parks but all the squares and
private gardens.   During the big frost of
1890–1 skylarks were seen every day searching
for food on the Thames Embankment.   These
strangers all vanish from London on the break-
up of the frost.

During the late autumn and winter months
a few large birds occasionally appear—heron,
mallard, widgeon, teal, &c. As a rule they
come and go during the dark hours. The sight
of water and the cries of the ornamental water-
fowl attract them. They are mostly irregular
visitors, and cannot very well be included in
the list of London birds.

The case of the black-headed gull is different,
as this species may now be classed with the
regular visitors, and not merely to the outlying
spaces, like the fieldfare, but to the central
parks of the metropolis, where, like the wood-
pigeon, he looks to man for food.

The black-headed gull has always been a
winter visitor in small numbers to the lower
reaches of the Thames, coming up the river as
far as London Bridge. In severe winters more
birds come; thus, in the winter of 1887–8 they
appeared in great numbers, and ranged as high
up as Putney. The late Mr. Tristram-Valentine,
in describing this visitation, wrote: 'It is seldom,
indeed, that these birds appeared in such
numbers in the Thames above London Bridge
as they have done lately, and their appearance
has, from its rarity, caused a corresponding

excitement among Londoners, as is proved by
the numbers of people that have crowded the
bridges and embankments to watch their movements.   To a considerable portion of these, no
doubt, the marvellous flight and power of wing
of the gull came as an absolute revelation.'

Gulls came up the river in still greater force
during the exceptionally long and severe frost
of 1892–3.   That was a memorable season in
the history of the London gulls.   Then, for the
last time, gulls were shot on the river between
the bridges, and this pastime put a stop to by
the police magistrates, who fined the sportsmen
for the offence of discharging firearms to the
public danger.   And then for the first time, so
far as I know, the custom of regularly feeding
the gulls in London had its beginning.   Every
day for a period of three to four weeks hundreds
of working men and boys would take advantage
of the free hour at dinner time to visit the
bridges and embankments, and give the scraps
left from their meal to the birds.   The sight
of this midday crowd hurrying down to the
waterside with welcome in their faces and food
in their hands must have come ' as an absolute
revelation ' to the gulls.

During the memorable frost of 1894–5 the birds again appeared in immense numbers, and would doubtless have soon left us, or else perished of cold and hunger on the snow-covered hummocks of ice which filled the Thames and gave it so arctic an aspect, but for the quantities of food cast to them every day. As in previous years when gulls have visited the Thames in considerable numbers, many of the birds found their way into the parks, and were especially numerous in St. James's Park, where they formed the habit of feeding with the ornamental water-fowl.

We have since experienced three exceptionally mild winters, so that the gulls were not driven by want to invade us ; but they have come to us nevertheless, not having forgotten the generous hospitality London extended to them in the frost. St. James's Park has now become the favourite wintering place of a considerable number of birds, and their habit is to spend the day on the lake, feeding on the broken bread and scraps of meat thrown to them from the bridge, and leaving about sunset to spend the night on the river. In the autumn of 1896, three or four days after the gulls began to

appear on the Thames, a body of two or three
hundred of these birds settled down in the
park water, and fed there every day and all
day long until the following spring—March
1897.

A favourite pastime of mine during the
winter months was to feed these park gulls with
sprats, which were plentiful and could be bought
anywhere for one penny a pound, or in quantities
for about a farthing the pound. Gulls cannot
live by bread alone ; it is true that even in
London they do not, like the blubber-eating
Greenlander, spew it out of their mouths, for
they will eat almost anything, but it is not
partaken of with zest, and even with a crop-full
they do not feel that they have dined. However
much bread they had had, no sooner would
they see the silvery gleam of a little tossed-up
sprat than there would be a universal scream of
excitement, a rush from all sides, and the whole
white vociferous crowd would be gathered before
me, almost brushing my face with their wings,
sweeping round and round, joyfully feasting on
the little fishes, cast to them in showers, to be
deftly caught before they touched the water.

Some of the birds, bolder or more intelligent

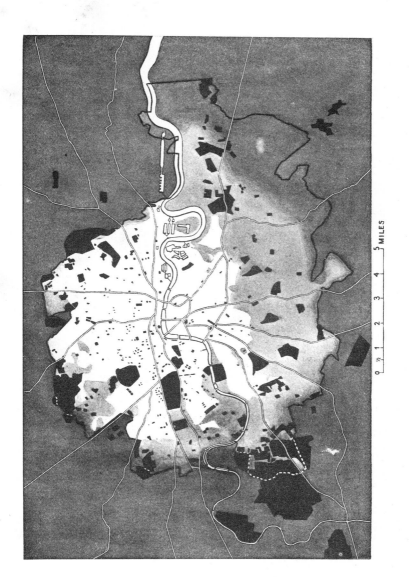

0   ½   1   2   3   4   5 MILES

VIEW ON HAMPSTEAD HEATH

than their fellows, would actually take the
sprats from the hand.

A very few days before writing this chapter
end, on January 30, 1898, I passed by the
water and saw the gulls there, where indeed
they have spent most of the daylight hours
since the first week in October. It was a rough
wild morning ; the hurrying masses of dark
cloud cast a gloom below that was like twilight ;
and though there was no mist the trees and
buildings surrounding the park appeared vague
and distant. The water, too, looked strange in
its intense blackness, which was not hidden by
the silver-grey light on the surface, for the surface was everywhere rent and broken by the
wind, showing the blackness beneath. Some of
the gulls—about 150 I thought—were on the
water together in a close flock, tailing off to a
point, all with their red beaks pointing one way
to the gale. Seeing them thus, sitting high as
their manner is, tossed up and down with the
tumbling water, yet every bird keeping his place
in the company, their whiteness and buoyancy
in that dark setting was quite wonderful. It
was a picture of black winter and beautiful wild
bird life which would have had a rare attraction

even in the desert places of the earth ; in
London it could not be witnessed without feelings of surprise and gratitude.

We see in this punctual return of the gulls,
bringing their young with them, that a new
habit has been acquired, a tradition formed,
which has given to London a new and exceedingly beautiful ornament, of more value than
many works of art.

CHAPTER IX

A SURVEY OF THE PARKS : WEST LONDON

A general survey of the metropolitan parks—West London—
Central parks, with Holland Park—A bird's highway—
Decrease of songsters—The thrush in Kensington Gardens—
Suggestions—Owls in Kensington Gardens—Other West
London open spaces—Ravenscourt Park as it was and as
it is.

OUR 'province' of London is happily not entirely
' covered with houses,' and in each of its six large
districts—West, North-west, North, East, South-
east, and South-west—there are many hundreds
of acres of green and tree-shaded spaces where the
Londoner may find a moderate degree of refreshment. Unfortunately for large masses of the
population, these spaces are very unequally
distributed, being mostly situated on or close
to the borderland, where town and country
meet; consequently they are of less value to
the dwellers in the central and densely peopled
districts than to the inhabitants of the suburbs,
who have pure air and ample healthy room
without these public grounds.

Before going the round of the parks, to note in detail their present condition and possibilities, chiefly with reference to their wild bird life, it would be well to take a rapid survey of the metropolitan open spaces generally. To enable the reader the more closely to follow me in the survey, I have introduced a map of the County of London on a small scale, in which the whole of the thickly built-over portion appears un-coloured; the surrounding country coloured green; the open spaces, including cemeteries, deep green; the small spaces—squares, graves, churchyards, gardens, recreation grounds, &c., as dark dots; the suburban districts, not densely populated, where houses have gardens and grounds, pale green.

Now the white space is not really birdless, being everywhere inhabited by sparrows, and in parts by numerous and populous colonies of semi-wild pigeons, while a few birds of other species make their homes in London gardens. Shirley Hibbert, writing of London birds in 1865, says : ' London is, indeed, far richer in birds than it deserves to be.' He also says : ' A few birds, however, appear to be specially adapted not merely for London as viewed from

without, but for London *par excellence*, that is
to say for the noisy, almost treeless City ; with

RAVENSCOURT
PARK

these   for
pioneers, nature
invades   the
Stock Exchange,
the   Court   of
Aldermen,   the
Bank, and all the railway termini, as
if to say, *Shut us out if you can.'* But
with the exception of these few peculiarly
urban species we may take it that the London

birds get their food, breed, and live most of the time in the open spaces where there are trees and bushes.   Even the starling, which breeds in buildings, must go to the parks to feed.

It must also be borne in mind that birds that penetrate into London from the surrounding country—those that, like the carrion crow, live on the borders and fly into or across London every day, migrants in spring and autumn, young birds reared outside of London going about in search of a place to settle in, and wanderers generally—all fly to and alight on the green spaces only.   These spaces form their camping grounds.   As there is annually a very considerable influx of feathered strangers, we can see by a study of the map how much easier to penetrate and more attractive some portions of the metropolis are than others.   It would simplify the matter still further if we were to look upon London as an inland sea, an archipelago, about fifty miles in circumference, containing a few very large islands, several of a smaller size, and numerous very small ones—a sea or lake with no well-defined shore-line, but mostly with wide borders which might be described as mixed land and water, with pro-

montories or tongues of land here and there
running into it. These promontories, also the
chains of islands, form, in some cases, broad
green thoroughfares along which the birds come ;
the sinuous band of the Thames also forms to
some extent a thoroughfare.

I believe it is a fact that in those parts of the
suburbs that are well timbered, and where the
houses have gardens and grounds, the bird
population is actually greater (with fewer
species) than in the country proper, even in
places where birds are very abundant. In parts
of Norwood, Sydenham, and Streatham, and the
neighbourhoods of Dulwich, Greenwich, Lee,
Highgate, and Hampstead, birds are extremely
abundant. Going a little further afield, on one
side of the metropolis we have Epping Forest,
and on the opposite side of the metropolis
several vast and well-wooded spaces abounding
in bird life—Kew Gardens, the Queen's private
grounds, Old Deer Park, Syon and Richmond
parks, Wimbledon, &c. From all these districts
there is doubtless a considerable overflow of
birds each season on to the adjacent country,
and into London, and some of the large parks
are well placed to attract these wanderers.

In going into a more detailed account of the
parks, it is not my intention to furnish anything
like a formal or guide-book description, assigning
a space to each, but, taking them as they come,
singly, in groups and chains, to touch or dwell
only on those points that chiefly concern us—
their characters, comparative advantages, and
their needs, with regard to bird life.   Beginning
with the central parks and other parks situated
in the West district, we will then pass to the
North-west and North districts, and so on until
the circle of the metropolis has been completed.

The central parks, Kensington Gardens and
Hyde Park, Green Park, and St. James's Park,
contain respectively 274, 360, 55, and 60 acres
—in round numbers 750 acres.   Add to this
Holland Park, the enclosed meadow-like grounds
adjoining Kensington Palace, Hyde Park Gardens,
St. George's burial-ground, and Buckingham
Palace Gardens, and we get altogether a total of
about nine hundred to one thousand acres of
almost continuous green country, extending
from High Street, Kensington, to Westminster.
This very large area (for to the eyes of the flying
bird it must appear as one) is favourably situated

to attract and support a very considerable amount of bird life. At its eastern extremity we see that it is close to the river, along which birds are apt to travel; while three miles and a half away, at its other end, it is again near the Thames, where the river makes a great bend near Hammersmith, and not very distant from the more or less green country about Acton.

There is no doubt that a majority of the summer visitants and wanderers generally that appear in the central parks come through Holland Park, as they are usually first observed in the shrubberies and trees at Kensington Palace. Holland Park, owing to its privacy and fine old trees, is a favourite resort of wild birds, and is indeed a better sanctuary than any public park in London. From the palace shrubberies the new-comers creep in along the Flower Walk, the Serpentine, and finally by way of the Green Park to St. James's Park. But they do not stay to breed, the place not being suitable for such a purpose. It is possible that a few find nesting-places in Buckingham Palace Gardens, and that others drift into Battersea Park.

Another proof that these parks—so sadly mismanaged from the bird-lover's point of view—

are situated advantageously may be found in the fact that three of the species which have established colonies in London within the last few years (wood-pigeon, moorhen, and dabchick) first formed settlements here, and from this centre have spread over the entire metropolis, and now inhabit every park and open space where the conditions are suited to their requirements. These three needed no encouragement : the summer visitors do certainly need it, and at Battersea, and in some other parks less than one fourth the size of Hyde Park, they find it, and are occasionally able to rear their young. Even the old residents, the sedentary species once common in the central parks, find it hard to maintain their existence ; they have died or are dying out. The missel-thrush, nuthatch, tree-creeper, oxeye, spotted woodpecker, and others vanished several years ago. The chaffinch was reduced to a single pair within the last few years ; this pair lingered on for a year or a little over, then vanished. Last spring, 1897, a few chaffinches returned, and their welcome song was heard in Kensington Gardens until June. Not a greenfinch is to be seen, the commonest and most prolific garden bird in England, so abundant that scores, nay hundreds, may be bought any Sunday morning in the autumn at the bird-dealers' shops in the slums of London, at about two pence per bird, or even less. The wrens a few years ago were reduced to a single pair, and had their nesting-place near the Albert Memorial; of the pair I believe one bird now remains. Two, perhaps three, pairs of hedge-sparrows inhabited Kensington Gardens during the summers of 1896 and 1897, but I do not think they succeeded in rearing any young. Nor did the one pair in St. James's Park hatch any eggs. In 1897 a pair of spotted flycatchers bred in Kensington Gardens, and were the only representatives of the summer visitors of the passerine order in all the central parks.

The robin has been declining for several years; a decade ago its sudden little outburst of bright melody was a common autumn and winter sound in some parts of the park, and in nearly all parts of Kensington Gardens. This delightful sound became less and less each season, and unless something is done will before many years cease altogether. The blue and cole tits are also now a miserable remnant, and are restricted to the gardens, where they may be seen, four or five together, on the high elms or clinging to the pendent twigs of the birches. The blackbird and song-thrush have also fallen very low; I do not believe that there are more than two dozen of these common birds in all this area of seven hundred and fifty acres. A larger number could be found in one corner of Finsbury Park. Finsbury and Battersea could each send a dozen or two of songsters as a gift to the royal West-end parks, and not miss their music.

Of all these vanishing species the thrush is most to be regretted, on account of its beautiful, varied, and powerful voice, for in so noisy an atmosphere as that of London loudness is a very great merit; also because (in London) this bird sings very nearly all the year round. Even at the present time how much these few remaining birds are to us! From one to two decades ago it was possible on any calm mild day in winter to listen to half a dozen thrushes singing at various points in the gardens; now it is very rare to hear more than one, and during the exceedingly mild winter of 1896–7 I never heard more than two. Even these few birds make a wonderful difference. There is a miraculous quality in their voice. In the best of many poems which the Poet Laureate has addressed to this, his favourite bird, he sings :

> Hearing thee first, who pines or grieves
> For vernal smiles and showers !
> Thy voice is greener than the leaves,
> And fresher than the flowers.

Even here in mid-London the effect is the same, and a strange glory fills the old ruined and deserted place. But, alas ! 'tis but an illusion, and is quickly gone. The tendency for many years past has been towards a greater artificiality. It saves trouble and makes for prettiness to cut down decaying trees. To take measures to prevent their fall, to drape them with ivy and make them beautiful in decay, would require some thought and care. It is not so long ago that Matthew Arnold composed his 'Lines written in Kensington Gardens.' It seems but the other day that he died ; but how impossible it would be for anyone to-day, at this spot, to experience the feeling which inspired those matchless verses !

In this lone, open glade I lie,
  Screened by deep boughs on either hand ;
And at its end, to stay the eye,
  Those black-crown'd, red-boled pine-trees stand !

Birds here make song, each bird has his,
  Across the girdling city's hum.
How green under the boughs it is !
  How thick the tremulous sheep-cries come !

Sometimes a child will cross the glade
  To take his nurse his broken toy ;
Sometimes a thrush flit overhead
  Deep in her unknown day's employ.

Here at my feet what wonders pass,
  What endless, active life is here !
What blowing daisies, fragrant grass !
  An air-stirr'd forest, fresh and clear.

        .   .   .   .

In the huge world, which roars hard by,
  Be others happy if they can !
But in my helpless cradle I
  Was breathed on by the rural Pan.

        .   .   .   .

Calm soul of all things !   Make it mine
  To feel amid the city's jar,
That there abides a peace of thine,
  Man did not make, and cannot mar.

The will to neither strive nor cry,
  The power to feel with others give !
Calm, calm me more ! nor let me die
  Before I have begun to live.

In these vast gardens and parks, with large trees, shrubberies, wide green spaces, and lakes, there should be ample room for many scores of the delightful songsters that are now vanishing or have already vanished. And much might be done, at a very small cost, to restore these species, and to add others.

One of the first and most important steps to be taken in order to make the central parks a suitable home for wild birds, especially of the songsters, both resident and migratory, that nest on or near the ground, is the exclusion of the army of cats that hunt every night and all night long in them. This subject will be discussed more fully in another chapter.

Proper breeding - places are also greatly wanted—close shrubberies and rockeries such as we find at Battersea and Finsbury Parks. The existing shrubberies give no proper shelter. In planting them the bird's need of privacy was not considered; the space allowed to them is too small, the species of plants that birds prefer to roost and nest in are too few. It would make a wonderful difference if in place of so many unsuitable exotic shrubs (especially of the ugly, dreary-looking rhododendron) we had more of the always pleasing yew and holly; also furze and bramble; with other native plants to be found in any country hedge, massed together in that charming disorder which men as well as birds prefer, although the gardeners do not know it. There are several spots in Kensington Gardens where masses of evergreens would look well and would form welcome refuges to scores of shy songsters.

The more or less open ground north of the Flower Walk forms a deep well-sheltered hollow, where it would be easy to create a small pond with rushes and osiers growing in it, which would be very attractive to the birds. It would be easy to make a spot in every park in London where the sedge-warbler could breed.

Another very much needed improvement is an island in the Serpentine, which would serve to attract wild birds. The Serpentine is by a good deal the largest of the artificial lakes of inner London, yet with the exception of a couple of moorhens, and in winter a stray gull or two

seen flying over the water, it has no wild bird
life, simply because there is no spot where a
wild bird can breed. The existing small island,
close to the north bank and the sub-rangers'
village, is used by some of the ducks to breed
in. Something might be done to make this island
more attractive to birds.

With one, perhaps two, exceptions, the comparatively large birds in the central parks have
been so fully written about in former chapters
that nothing more need be said of them in this
place. It remains only to speak of the owls in
Kensington Gardens.

It is certainly curious to find that in these
gardens, where, as we have seen, birds are not
encouraged, two such species as the jackdaw
and owl are still resident, although long vanished
from all their other old haunts in London. Of
so important a bird as the owl I should have
preferred to write at some length in one of the
earlier chapters, but there was very little to say,
owing to its rarity and secrecy. Nor could it
be included in the chapters on recent colonists,
since it is probable that it has always been an
inhabitant of Kensington Gardens, although its
existence there has not been noticed by those

who have written on the wild bird life of London.
It is unfortunate that we have no enjoyment of
our owls : they hide from sight in the old hollow
trees, and when they occasionally exercise their
voices at night we are not there to hear them.
Still, it is a pleasure to know that they are there,
and probably always have been there.   It is
certain that during the past year both the brown
and white owl have been living in the gardens,
as the night-watchers hear the widely different
vocal performances of both birds, and have also
seen both species.   Probably there are not more
than two birds of each kind.   Owls have the
habit of driving away their young, and the stray
white owls occasionally seen or heard in various
parts of London may be young birds driven from
the gardens.   Some time ago the cries of a white
owl were heard on several nights at Lambeth
Palace, and it was thought that the bird had
made its home in the tower of Lambeth Church,
close by.   In the autumn of 1896 a solitary
white owl frequented the trees at Buckhurst
Hill.   An ornithological friend told me that he
had seen an owl, probably the same bird, one
evening flying over the Serpentine ; and on
inquiring of some of the park people, I was

told that they knew nothing about an owl, but that a cockatoo had mysteriously appeared every evening at dusk on one of the trees near the under-ranger's lodge! After a few weeks it was seen no more. I fancy that this owl had been expelled 'from the gardens by its parents.

Directly in line with the central and Holland parks, about a mile and a quarter west of Holland Park, we have Ravenscourt Park—the last link of a broken chain. To the birds that come and go it occupies the position of a half-way house between the central parks and the country proper. Unhappily West Kensington, which lies between Holland and Ravenscourt Parks, is now quite covered with houses—a brand-new yet depressing wilderness of red brick, without squares, gardens, boulevards, or breathing spaces of any description whatsoever. Away on the right hand and on the left a few small green spaces are found—on one hand Shepherd's Bush Green, and on the other Brook Green, St. Paul's Schools ornamental grounds, and Hammersmith Cemetery and Cricket Ground. But from West Kensington it is far for children's feet to a spot of green turf.

Ravenscourt, though not large (32 acres), is very beautiful. With Waterlow, Clissold, and Brockwell Parks it shares the distinction of being a real park, centuries old; and despite the new features, the gravelled paths, garden-beds, iron railings, &c., which had to be introduced when it was opened to the public, it retains much of its original park-like character. Its venerable elms, hornbeams, beeches, cedars, and hawthorns are a very noble possession. To my mind this indeed is the most beautiful park in London, or perhaps I should say that it *would* be the most beautiful if the buildings round it were not so near and conspicuous. It may be that I am somewhat prejudiced in its favour. I knew it when it was private, and the old image is very vivid to memory; I lived for a long time beside it in sad days, when the constant sight of such a green and shady wilderness from my window was a great consolation. It was beautiful even in the cold, dark winter months when it was a waste of snow, and when, despite the bitter weather, the missel-thrush poured out its loud triumphant notes from the top of a tall elm. In its spring and summer aspect it had a wild grace and freshness, which

made it unlike any other spot known to me
in or near London. The old manor house inside the park was seldom occupied; no human
figure was visible in the grounds; there were
no paths, and all things grew untended. The
grass was everywhere long, and in spring lit
with colour of myriads of wild flowers; from
dawn to dusk its shady places were full of the
melody of birds; exquisitely beautiful in its
dewy and flowery desolation, it was like a home
of immemorial peace, the one remnant of
unadulterated nature in the metropolis.

The alterations that had to be made in this
park when the County Council took it over
produced in me an unpleasant shock; and the
birds were also seriously affected by the change.
When the gates were thrown open, in 1888, and
a noisy torrent of humanity poured in and
spread itself over their sweet sanctuary, they
fled in alarm, and for a time the park was
almost birdless. The carrion crows, strange to
say, stuck to their nesting-tree, and by-and-by
some of the deserters began to return, to be
followed by others, and now there is as much
bird life as in the old days. It is probable,
however, that some of the summer visitors have

ceased to breed.   At present we have the
crow, wood-pigeon, missel-thrush, chaffinch,
wren, hedge-sparrow, and in the summer the
pied wagtail and spotted flycatcher and willow-
wren.

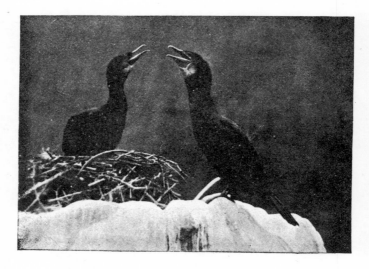

CORMORANTS AT ST. JAMES'S PARK

CHAPTER X

NORTH-WEST AND NORTH LONDON

BEFORE proceeding to give a brief account of the parks and open spaces of North-west and North London it is necessary to mention here a group of open spaces just within the West district, on its northern border, a mile and a half to two miles north of Ravenscourt Park. These are Wormwood Scrubs, Little Wormwood Scrubs, Old Oak Common, and Kensal Green Cemetery. As they contain altogether not far short of three hundred acres, and are in close proximity, they might in time have been thrown into one park. A large open space will be

sadly needed in that part of London before
many years are passed, and it is certain that
West London cannot go on burying its dead
much longer at Kensal Green.   But it is to be
feared that the usual short-sighted policy will
prevail with regard to these spaces, and a good
deal of the space known as Old Oak Common
has already been enclosed with barbed-wire
fences, and it is now said that the commoners'
rights in this space have been extinguished.

Beyond these spaces are Acton and Harlesden
—a district where town and country mix.

From Wormwood Scrubs to Regent's Park
it is three miles as the crow flies—three miles of
houses inhabited by a working-class population,
with no green spot except the Paddington
Recreation Ground, which is small (25 acres),
and of little or no use to the thousands of poor
children in this vast parish, being too far from
their homes.

Crossing the line dividing the West from the
North-west district near Kensal Green, we find
the following four not large open spaces in
Kilburn—Kensal Rise, Brondesbury Park (pri-
vate), Paddington Cemetery, and Kilburn or
Queen's Park (30 acres).

All this part of London is now being rapidly covered with houses, and the one beautiful open space, with large old trees in it, is Brondesbury Park. How sad to think that this fine park will probably be built over within the next few years, and that the only public open space left will be the Queen's Park—a dreary patch of stiff clay, where the vegetation is stunted and looks tired of life. Even a few exceptionally dirty-looking sparrows that inhabit it appear to find it a depressing place.

Two miles east of this melancholy spot is Regent's Park, which now forms one continuous open space, under one direction, with Primrose Hill, and contains altogether 473 acres. It is far and away the largest of the inner London parks, its area exceeding that of Hyde Park by 112 acres. Its large extent is but one of its advantages. Although not all free to the public, it is all open to the birds, and the existence of several more or less private enclosed areas is all in their favour. On its south, east, and west sides this space has the brick wilderness of London, an endless forest of chimneys defiling the air with their smoke ; but on the north side it touches a district where gardens abound, and trees, shrubs, and luxuriant ivy and creepers give it a country-like aspect. This pleasant green character is maintained until Hampstead Heath and the country proper is reached, and over this rural stretch of North-west London the birds come and go freely between the country and Regent's Park. This large space should be exceedingly attractive to all such birds as are not intolerant of a clay soil. There are extensive green spaces, a good deal of wood, and numerous large shrubberies, which are more suitable for birds to find shelter and breed in than the shrubberies in the central parks. There is also a large piece of ornamental water, with islands, and, better still, the Regent's Canal running for a distance of nearly one mile through the park. The steeply sloping banks on one side, clothed with rank grass and shrubs and crowned with large unmutilated trees, give this water the appearance of a river in the country, and it is, indeed, along the canal where birds are always most abundant, and where the finest melody may be heard. All these advantages should make Regent's Park as rich in varied bird life as any open space in the metropolis. Unfortunately the birds are not encouraged, and if this park was not so large, and so placed as to be in some degree in touch with the country, it would be in the same melancholy condition as Hyde Park. The species now found are the blackbird and thrush, greenfinch (rare) and chaffinch, robin, dunnock, and wren (the last very rare), and in summer two or three migrants are added. But most of the birds find it hard to rear any young owing to the birds'-nesting boys and loafers, who are not properly watched, and to the cats that infest the shrubberies. Even by day cats have the liberty of this park. Wood-pigeons come in numbers to feed in the early morning, and a few pairs build nests, but as a rule their eggs are taken. Carrion crows from North London visit the park on most days, and make occasional incursions into the Zoological Gardens, where they are regarded with very unfriendly feelings. They go there on the chance of picking up a crumb or two dropped from the tables of the pampered captives; and perhaps for a peep at the crow-house, where many corvines from many lands may be seen turning their eyes skyward, uttering at the same time a cry of recognition, to watch the sweeping flight of their passing relatives, who ' mock them with their loss of liberty.'

The water-birds (wild) are no better off in this park than the songsters in the shrubberies, yet it could easily be made more attractive and safe as a breeding-place. As it is, the dabchick seldom succeeds in hatching eggs, and even the semi-domestic and easily satisfied moorhen finds it hard to rear any young.

The other great green space in the North-west district is Hampstead Heath, which contains, including Parliament Hill and other portions acquired in recent years, 507 acres. On its outer border it touches the country, in parts a very beautiful country ; while on its opposite side it abuts on London proper, forming on the south and south-east the boundary of an unutterably dreary portion of the metropolis, a congeries of large and densely-populated parishes—Kentish and Camden Towns, Hollo-way, Highbury, Canonbury, Islington, Hoxton : thousands of acres of houses, thousands of miles of streets, vast thoroughfares full of trams and traffic and thunderous noises, interminable roads, respectable and monotonous, and mean streets and squalid streets innumerable. Here, then, we have a vast part of London, which is like the West-central and East-central districts in that it is without any open space, except the comparatively insignificant one of Highbury Fields. It is to the Heath that the inhabitants of all this portion of London must go for fresh air and verdure; but the distance is too great for most people, and the visits are consequently made on Sundays and holidays in summer. Even this restricted use they are able to make of 'London's playing ground,' or 'Happy Hampstead,' as it is lovingly called, must have a highly beneficial effect on the health, physical and moral, of the people.

To come to the bird life of this largest of London's open spaces. Owing to its very openness and large extent, which makes it impossible for the constables to keep a watch on the visitors, especially on the gangs of birds'-nesting boys and young men who make it a happy hunting-ground during the spring and summer months, the Heath is in reality a very unfavourable breeding-place for birds. Linnets, yellow-hammers, chaffinches, robins, several warblers, and other species nest every year, but probably very rarely succeed in bringing up their young. Birds are nevertheless numerous and in great variety: the large space and its openness attract them, while all about the Heath large private gardens, woods, and preserves exist, which are perfect sanctuaries for most small birds and some large species. There is a small rookery on some elm-trees at the side of the High Street; and another close to the Heath, near Golder's Hill, on the late Sir Spencer Wells's property. And in other private grounds the carrion crow, daw, wood-pigeon, stock-dove, turtle-dove, white owl, and wood owl, green and lesser spotted woodpecker still breed. The corncrake is occasionally heard. The following small birds, summer visitors, breed on the Heath or in the adjacent private grounds, especially in Lord Mansfield's beautiful woods : wryneck and cuckoo, grasshopper-, sedge- and reed-warblers, blackcap and garden warbler, both whitethroats, wood and willow wrens, chiffchaff, redstart, stonechat, pied wagtail, tree-pipit, red-backed shrike, spotted flycatcher, swallow, house martin, swift, and goldfinch. Wheatears visit the Heath on passage ; fieldfares may be seen on most days throughout the winter, and occasionally redwings ; also the redpole, siskin, and the grey wagtail. The resident small birds include most of the species to be found in the county of Middlesex. The bullfinch and the hawfinch are rare.

My young friend, Mr. E. C. H. Moule, who is a keen observer, has very kindly sent me his notes on the birds of Hampstead, made during a year's residence on the edge of the Heath, and taking his list with my own, and comparing them with the list made by Mr. Harting, published in Lobley's ' Hampstead Hill' in 1885, it appears that there have been very few changes in the bird population of this district during the last decade.

It would be difficult to make the Heath itself a safer breeding-place for the birds, resident and migratory, that inhabit it. The only plan would be to establish small sanctuaries at suitable spots. Unfortunately these would have to be protected from the nest-robbers by spiked iron railings, and that open wild appearance of the Heath, which is its principal charm, would be spoiled.

With the ponds something can be done. There are a good number of them, large and small, some used for bathing in summer, and all for skating in winter, but so far nothing has been done to make them attractive to the birds ; and it may be added that a few beds of rushes and other aquatic plants for cover, which would make them suitable habitations for several species of birds, would also greatly add to their beauty. How little would have to be done to give life and variety to these somewhat desolate-looking pieces of water, may be seen on the Heath itself. One of the smallest is the Leg of Mutton Pond, on the West Heath, a rather muddy pool where dogs are accustomed to bathe. At its narrow end it has a small bed of bulrushes, which has been inhabited by a pair of moorhens for several years past. They are very tame, and appear quite unconcerned in the presence of people standing on the margin to gaze at and admire them, and of the dogs barking and splashing about in the water a few yards away. There is no wire netting to divide their own little domain from the dogs' bathing place, and no railing on the bank. Yet here they live all the year round very contentedly, and rear brood after brood of young every summer. Here, as in other places, it has been observed that the half-grown young birds assist their parents in building a second nest and in rearing the new brood, and it has also been re-marked that when the young are fully grown the old birds drive them from the pond. There is room for only one pair in that small patch of rushes, and they know it. The driven-out young wander about in search of a suitable spot to settle in, but find no place on the Heath. Pro-bably some of them spend the winter in Lord Mansfield's woods. A gentleman residing in the neighbourhood told me that at the end of the short frost in January 1897, when the ice was melted, he saw one morning a large number of moorhens, between thirty and forty, feeding in the meadow near the ponds in Lord Mansfield's grounds.

I have been told that no rushes have been planted on the Heath, and nothing done to en-courage wild birds to settle at the ponds, simply because it has never occurred to anyone in autho-rity, and no person has ever suggested that it would be a good thing to do. Now that the sug-gestion is made, let us hope that it will receive consideration. I fancy that every lover of nature would agree that a pair or two of quaint pretty moorhens ; a pair of lively dabchicks, diving, uttering that long, wild, bubbling cry that is so pleasant to hear, and building their floating nest ; and perhaps a sedge-warbler for ever playing on that delightful little barrel-organ of his, would give more pleasure than the pair of monotonous mute swans to be seen on some of the ponds, looking very uncomfortable, much too big for such small sheets of water, and altogether out of harmony with their surroundings.

With the exception of this omission, the management of the Heath by the County Council has so far been worthy of all praise. The trees recently planted will add greatly to the beauty and value of this space, which contains open ground enough for all the thousands that visit it in summer to roam about and take their sun-bath.

Near the Heath, on its east side, in the North London district, we have a group of four highly attractive open spaces. They are ranged in pairs at some distance apart. One pair is Highgate Woods (70 acres) and Churchyard Bottom Wood (52 acres), not yet open to the public ; the second pair is Waterlow Park (26 acres) and Highgate Cemetery (40 acres). The two first have a special value in their rough, wild, woodland character, wherein they differ from all other open spaces in or near London. But although these spaces are both wildernesses, and so close together as to be almost touching, they each have an individual character. A very large portion of the space called Highgate Woods is veritably a wood, very thick and copse-like, so that to turn aside from the path is to plunge into a dense thicket of trees and saplings, where a lover of solitude might spend a long summer's day without seeing a human face. Owing to this thick growth it is impossible for the few guardians of this space to keep a watch on the mischievous visitors, with the result that in summer birds'-nesting goes on with impunity; the evil, however, cannot well be remedied if the woods are to be left in their present state. It would certainly greatly add to their charm if such species as inhabit woods of this character were to be met with here—the woodpeckers, the kestrel and sparrow-hawk and the owls, that have not yet forsaken this part of London; and the vociferous jay, shrieking with anger at being disturbed; and the hawfinch, with his metallic clicking note ; and the minute, arrow-shaped, long-tailed tits that stream through the upper branches in a pretty procession. But even the warmest friend to the birds would not like to see these woods thinned and cut through with innumerable roads, and the place changed from a wilderness to an artificial garden or show park.

The adjoining Churchyard Bottom Wood is the wildest and most picturesque spot in North London, with an uneven surface, hill and valley, a small stream running through it, old unmutilated trees of many kinds scattered about in groups and groves, and everywhere masses of bramble and furze. It is quite unspoiled, in character a mixture of park and wild, rough common, and wholly delightful. Indeed, it is believed to be a veritable fragment—the only one left—of the primæval forest of Middlesex.

It is earnestly to be hoped that the landscape gardener will not be called in to prepare this place for the reception of the public—the improver on nature, whose conventional mind is only concerned with a fine show of fashionable blooms, whose highest standard is the pretty, cloying artificiality of Kew Gardens. Let him loose here, and his first efforts will be directed to the rooting up of the glorious old gorse and bramble bushes, and the planting of exotic bushes in their place, especially the monotonous rhododendron, that dreary plant the sight of which oppresses us like a nightmare in almost every public park and garden and open space in the metropolis.

Waterlow Park, although small, is extremely interesting, and contains a good amount of large well-grown timber ; it is, in fact, one of the real old parks which have been spared to us in London. It is indeed a beautiful and refreshing spot, and being so small and so highly popular, attracting crowds of people every day throughout the summer months, it does not afford a very favourable breeding-place for birds. Nevertheless, the number of songsters of various species is not small, for it is not as if these had no place but the park to breed in ; the town in this district preserves something of its rural character, and the bird population of the northern portion of Highgate is, like that of Hampstead, abundant and varied. There is also the fact to be borne in mind that Waterlow Park is one of two spaces that join, the park being divided from the cemetery by a narrow lane or footpath. To the birds these two spaces form one area.

Of Highgate Cemetery it is only necessary to say, in passing, that its 'manifest destiny' is to be made one open space for the public with its close neighbour; that from this spot you have the finest view of the metropolis to be had from the northern heights ; and when there are green leaves in place of a forest of headstones, and a few large trees where monstrous mausoleums and monuments of stone now oppress the earth, the ground will form one of the most beautiful open spaces in London.

There are two little lakes in Waterlow Park where some ornamental fowls are kept, and of these lakes, or ponds, it may be said, as of the Hampstead ponds, that they are too small for such a giant as the mute swan. On the Thames and on large sheets of water the swan is a great ornament, his stately form and whiteness being very attractive to the eye. On the small ponds he is apt to get his plumage very dirty and to be a mischievous bird. He requires space to move about and look well in, and water-weeds to feed on. It is not strange to find that our small, interesting, wild aquatic birds have not succeeded in colonising in this park.

A mile and a half east of Waterlow Park there is the comparatively large park, containing an area of 115 acres, which was foolishly misnamed Finsbury Park by the Metropolitan Board of Works. It is the largest and most important open space in North London, and with the exception of that of Battersea is the best of all the newly-made parks of the metropolis. It promises, indeed, to be a very fine place, but its oldest trees have only been planted twenty-eight years, and have not yet attained to a majestic size. There is one feature which will always to some extent spoil the beauty of this spot—namely, the exceedingly long, straight, monotonous Broad Walk, planted with black poplars, where the trees are all uniform in size and trimmed to the same height from the ground. Should it ever become necessary to cut down a large number of trees in London for fuel, or for the construction of street defences, or some other purpose, it is to be hoped that the opportunity will be seized to get rid of this unsightly avenue.

The best feature in this park is the very
large extent of well-planted shrubberies, and it
is due to the shelter they afford that blackbirds
and thrushes are more abundant here than in
any other open space in the metropolis, not even
excepting that paradise of birds, Battersea Park.
It is delightful to listen to such a volume of
bird music as there is here morning and evening
in spring and summer.   Even in December and
January, on a dull cold afternoon with a grey
smoky mist obscuring everything, a concert of
thrushes may be heard in this park with more
voices in it than would be heard anywhere in
the country.   The birds are fed and sheltered
and protected when breeding, and they are
consequently abundant and happy.   What
makes all this music the more remarkable is the
noisiness of the neighbourhood.   The park is
surrounded by railway lines ; trains rush by with
shrieks and earth-shaking thunder every few
moments, and the adjoining thoroughfare of
Seven Sisters Road is full of the loud noises of
traffic.   Here, more than anywhere in London,
you are reminded of Milton's description of the
jarring and discordant grating sounds at the
opening of hell's gates ; and one would imagine

that in such an atmosphere the birds would become crazed, and sing, if they sang at all, 'like sweet bells jangled, out of tune and harsh.' But all this noise troubles them not at all ; they sing as sweetly here, with voices just as pure and rapturous, as in any quiet country lane or wood.

DABCHICK FEEDING ITS YOUNG

The other most common wild birds are the robin, tits, starling, dabchick, and moorhen. The chaffinch, greenfinch, hedge-sparrow, and wren are less common.

Half a mile to the east of Finsbury Park we have Clissold Park (53 acres), comparatively small but singularly attractive. This is one of the old and true parks that have remained to London, and, like Ravenscourt and Brockwell, it has an old manor house standing in it; and this building, looking upon water and avenues of noble elms and wide green spaces, gives it the appearance of a private domain rather than a public place. Close by is Abney Park Cemetery, which is now so crammed with corpses as to make it reasonable to indulge the hope that before long it will be closed as a burial place, only to be re-opened as a breathing space for the living. And as the distance which separates these two spaces is not great, let us indulge the further hope that it may be found possible to open a way between them to make them one park of not less than about a hundred acres.

Clissold Park is specially interesting to bird lovers in London on account of the efforts of the superintendent and the park constables in encouraging and protecting the bird life of the place. In writing of the carrion crow, the jackdaw, and the little grebe, I have spoken of this park, and shall have occasion to speak of it again in a future chapter.

South of Clissold, with the exception of the

strip of green called Highbury Fields, there is
no open space nearer than St. James's Park, four
miles distant. Highbury Fields (27 acres) was
opened to the public about twelve years ago,
and although small and badly shaped, it is by
no means an unimportant ' lung ' of North
London. To the inhabitants of Highbury,
Canonbury, and Islington it is the nearest open
space, and though in so vast and populous an
area, is a refreshing and pretty spot, with good
shrubberies and healthy well-grown young trees.
A few years ago a small rookery existed at the
northern extremity of the ground, where some
old trees are still standing, but the birds have
left, it is said on account of the decay of their
favourite tree. Skylarks also bred here up to
the time of the opening of the ground to the
public. The only wild birds at present, after the
sparrows, are the starlings that come in small
flocks, and a few occasional visitors. A few
years ago it was proposed to make a pond : I
fear that the matter has been forgotten, or that
all the good things there were to give have been
bestowed on the show parks, leaving nothing for
poor Highbury and Islington.

CHAPTER XI

EAST LONDON

JUDGING solely from the map, with its sprinkling
of green patches, one might be led to suppose
that East London is not worse off than other
metropolitan districts in the matter of open
spaces.   The truth is that it is very much worse
off; and it might almost be said that for the
mass of East-enders there are practically no
breathing spaces in that district.   The population is about a million, the greatest portion of
it packed into the parishes which border on the
river and the East Central district; that is to
say, on all that part of London which is most

destitute of open spaces. In all this poor and overcrowded part of the East the tendency has been to get more and more housing-room out of the ground, with the result that not only have the old gardens vanished but even the mean back-yards have been built over, and houses densely packed with inmates stand back to back, or with little workshops between. One can but wonder that this deadly filling-up process has been permitted to go on by the authorities. It is plain that the people who live in such conditions, whose lives are passed in small stuffy rooms, with no outside space but the foul-smelling narrow dusty streets, are more in need of open spaces than the dwellers in other districts ; yet to most of them even Victoria Park is practically as distant, as inaccessible, as Hyde Park, or Hampstead Heath, or the country proper. If once in many days a man is able to get away for needed change and refreshment, he finds it as easy to go to Epping Forest as to Victoria Park and Hackney Marsh ; but it is not on many days in the year, in some cases not on any day, that he can take his wife and children.

The open spaces of the East district, which

(excepting those distant spaces situated on the borders of Epping Forest) are all near together and form a large circular group, are Hackney Downs, London Fields, Victoria Park with Hackney Common, and Hackney Marsh with South and North Mill Fields—about 730 acres in all. These grounds, as we have seen, are too distant to be of much benefit to the larger part of the population, and, it may be added, they have not the same value as breathing spaces as the parks and commons in other London districts. Victoria Park does not refresh a man like Hampstead Heath, nor even like Hyde Park. The atmosphere is not the same. You are not there out of the smoke and smells and gloom of East London. The atmosphere of Hackney Marsh is better, but the distance is greater, and the Marsh is not a place where women and children can rest in the shade, since shade there is none.

To begin with the spaces nearest to the boundary line of North London : we have the two isolated not large spaces of Hackney Downs (41 acres) and London Fields (26 acres). These are green recreation grounds with few trees or shrubs, where birds cannot breed and do not live. Hackney Downs is, however, used as a feeding ground by a few thrushes and other birds that inhabit some of the adjacent private gardens where there are trees and shrubs.

Victoria Park contains 244 acres, to which may be added the 20 acres of Hackney Common, and is rather more than two-thirds as large as Hyde Park. Having been in existence for upwards of twenty years, it is one of the oldest of our new parks, and is important on account of its large size, also because it is the only park in the most populous metropolitan district.

If it were possible to view it with the East-enders' eyes—eyes accustomed to prospects so circumscribed and to so unlovely an aspect of things—it might seem like a paradise, with its wide green spaces, its groves and shrubberies, and lakes and wooded islands. To the dwellers in West and South-west London it has a somewhat depressing appearance, a something almost of gloom, as if Nature herself in straying into such a region had put off her brilliance and freshness to be more in tune with her human children. The air is always more or less smoke-laden in that part. That forest of innumerable chimneys, stretching away miles and miles over all that

desolate overcrowded district to the river, and
the vast parishes of Rotherhithe, Bermondsey,
and Deptford beyond it, to the City and
Islington and Kingsland on the north side, dims
the atmosphere with an everlasting cloud of
smoke; and Victoria Park is on most days
under it. On account of this smokiness of
the air the trees, although of over twenty years'
growth, are not large—not nearly so large as
the much younger trees in Battersea Park.
Trees and shrubs have a somewhat grimy
appearance, and even the grass is not so green
as in other places.

Among the recent bird-colonists of London,
we find that the moorhen and ringdove have
established themselves here, but in very small
numbers. There are two good-sized lakes
(besides a bathing-pond), and the islands might
be made very attractive to birds, both land and
water. They are planted with trees, the best
grown in the park, but have no proper cover
for species that nest on the ground and in low
bushes, and no rushes or other aquatic plants on
their edges. It is a wonder that even the moorhens are able to rear any young. The lakes are
much used for boating, and this is said to be in

the way of providing the birds with proper
refuges in and round the islands; but there is
no lake in London more used for boating exercise than that of Battersea, yet it has there been
found possible to give proper accommodation
and protection to the water-birds in the breeding
season.

It is melancholy to find that the songsters
have been decreasing in this park for some years
past. Birds are perhaps of more value here than
in any other metropolitan open space. Thrushes,
blackbirds, and chaffinches are still not uncommon. The robin, titmouse, and dunnock
are becoming rare. The greenfinch and (I
believe) the wren have vanished. The decrease
of the chaffinch is most regretted by the East-
enders, who have an extraordinary admiration
for that bird. Bird fanciers are very numerous
in the East, and the gay chaffinch is to them
the first of the feathered race; in fact, it may
be said that he is first and the others nowhere.
Now the value of the chaffinch to the bird
fancier depends on his song—on the bird's readi-
ness to sing when his music is wanted, and the
qualities of his notes, their strength, spirit, and
wildness. In the captive state the song

deteriorates unless the captive is frequently made to hear and sing against a wild bird. At these musical contests the caged bird catches and retains something of the fine passion and brilliancy of his wild antagonist, and the more often he is given such a lesson the better will it be for its owner, who may get twenty to fifty shillings, and sometimes much more, for a good singer. Victoria Park was the only accessible place to most of the East-enders who keep chaffinches for singing-matches and for profit, to which their birds could be taken to get the necessary practice. To this park they were accustomed to come in considerable numbers, especially on Sunday mornings in spring and summer. Even now, when the wild birds are so greatly reduced in numbers, many chaffinch fanciers may be met with; even on working days I have met as many as a dozen men slouching about among the shrubberies, each with a small cage covered with a cotton handkerchief or rag, in quest of a wild bird for his favourite to challenge and sing against. They do not always succeed in finding their wild bird, and when found he may not be a first-rate singer, or may become alarmed and fly away; and as it is a far cry to Epping Forest and the country, most of the men being very poor and having some occupation which takes up most of their time, the decline of Victoria Park as a training ground for their birds is a great loss to them.

I have tried, but without success, to believe that there was something more than the sporting or gambling spirit in the East-ender's passion for the chaffinch. Is it not probable, I have asked myself, that this short swift lyric, the musical cry of a heart overflowing with gladness, yet with a ring of defiance in it, a challenge to every other chaffinch within hearing, has some quality in it which stirs a human hearer too, even an East-ender, more than any other bird sound, and suddenly wakes that ancient wild nature that sleeps in us, the vanished sensations of gladness and liberty? I am reluctantly compelled to answer that I think not. The East-ender admires the chaffinch because he is a sporting bird—a bird that affords good sport; just as the man who has been accustomed to shoot starlings from traps has a peculiar fondness for that species, and as the cock-fighter admires the gamecock above all feathered creatures. Deprive the cock-fighter of his sport —the law has not quite succeeded in taking it away yet—and the bird ceases to attract him; its brilliant courage, the beauty of its shape, its scarlet comb, shining red hackles and green sickle plumes, and its clarion voice that proclaims in the dark silent hours that another day has dawned, all go for nothing.

It is unhappily necessary to say even more in derogation of the East-end chaffinch fancier, who strikes one as nothing worse than a very quiet inoffensive person, down on his luck, as he goes softly about among the shrubberies with the little tied-up cage under his arm. He is not always looking out for a wild chaffinch solely for the purpose of affording his pet a little practice in the art of singing; he not unfrequently carries a dummy chaffinch and a little bird-lime concealed about his person, and is quick and cunning at setting up his wooden bird and limed twigs when a wild bird appears and the park constable is out of sight.

In some of the parks, where the wild birds are cared for, the men who are found skulking about the shrubberies with cages in their hands are very sharply ordered out. It is not so in Victoria Park, and this may be the reason of the decrease in its wild bird life.

In Victoria Park I have met with some amusing instances of the entire absorption of the chaffinch votaries in their favourite bird, their knowledge of and quickness in hearing and seeing him, and inability to see and hear any other species. Thus, one man assured me that he had never seen a robin in the park, that there were no robins there. Another related as a very curious thing that he had seen a robin, red breast and all, and had heard it sing ! Yet you can see and hear a robin in Victoria Park any day.

We now come to the famous Marsh. Victoria Park is in shape like a somewhat gouty or swollen leg and foot, the leg cut off below the knee ; the broad toes of the foot point towards London Fields and the north, the flat sole towards Bishopsgate Street, distant two miles ; the upper part of the severed leg almost touches the large space of Hackney Marsh. The Marsh contains 337 acres ; the adjoining North and South Mill Fields 23 and 34 acres respectively— the whole thus comprising an area of nearly

400 acres. It was acquired by the London
County Council for the public in 1894, but
before its acquisition the East-end public had
the use of it, and, no doubt, some right in it, as
the owners of ponies and donkeys were accustomed to keep their animals there. It was a
kind of no-man's-land in London, and it is
indeed with the greatest bitterness that the old
frequenters of the Marsh of (to them) pleasant
memories recall the liberty they formerly
enjoyed in following their own devices, and
compare it with the restrictions of the present
time. There is no liberty now, they complain.
If a man sits down on the grass a policeman
will come and look at him to see if he is doing
any damage. The County Council have deprived
the public of its ancient sacred rights. It must
be borne in mind that the ' public ' spoken of
by the discontented ones means only a small
section, and not the most reputable section, of
the very large population of East London.

To those who know Hackney Marsh from
having looked upon it from a railway carriage
window (and most of the dwellers in other
districts know it only in that way) it is but a
green, flat, low piece of land, bounded by

buildings of some kind in the distance, a feature-
less space over which the vision roams in vain
in search of something to rest upon, utterly
devoid of interest, to be seen and straightway
forgotten. Yet I have experienced a pleasing
sense of exhilaration here, a feeling somewhat
differing in character from that produced in
me by any other metropolitan open space. And
this was not strange, for there is really nothing
like Hackney Marsh in London. Commons,
indeed, of various aspects we have in plenty,
parks, too, natural, artificial, dreary, pretty ; and
heaths, downs, woods, and wildernesses ; but the
Marsh alone presents to the eyes a large expanse
of absolutely flat grassy land, without a bush,
stick, or molehill to break its smooth surface.
A mile or a mile and a quarter away, according
to the direction, you see an irregular line of
buildings forming the horizon, with perhaps a
tapering church spire and a tall factory chimney
or two ; and if this extent of green waste seems
not great, it should be borne in mind that a man
standing on a flat surface has naturally a very
limited horizon, and that a mile in this district
of London is equal to two miles or more in the
country, owing to the blue haze which produces

an illusive effect of distance. Walking about this green level land in pleasant weather, I have experienced in some degree the delightful sensation which is always produced in us by a perfectly flat extensive surface, such as we find in some parts of Cambridgeshire, Lincolnshire, and Norfolk. This is the individual character and peculiar fascination of Hackney Marsh. And it is possible that this feeling of liberty and ease, which mere flatness and spaciousness give, was an element in the attraction which the Marsh has always had for the East Londoner.

Here on a windy day at the end of February I have been tempted to exclaim (like a woman), ' What a picture I could make—if I only knew how to paint ! ' The rains and floods and spring-like warmth of the winter of 1896–7 had made the grass look preternaturally green ; the distant buildings, ugly perhaps when viewed closely, at the distance of a mile, or even half a mile, were looking strangely picturesque in the pale smoky haze, changing, when the sun was obscured by a flying cloud and again burst forth, from deep blue to bright pearly grey; and the tall chimneys changed, too, from a darkness that was almost black to glowing brick-red. The wind was so strong that it was a labour to walk against it; but as I walked along the river I came on a solitary swan, and as though alarmed he rose up and flew away before me with a very free powerful flight in the face of the wind; but he flew low, and for a distance of a quarter of a mile his white wings shining in the sun looked wonderfully bright and beautiful against the vivid green expanse. The swans in this part of the River Lea are the property of the Water Company, but they fly about very freely, and are like wild birds. Larks, too, were soaring to sing on that day in spite of the wind's violence; first one fluttered up before me, then a second, then a third, and by-and-by I had four high overhead within hearing at the same time. It struck me as a great thing to hear four larks at one time in a metropolitan open space, for the lark is fast dying out in the neighbourhood of London. I greatly doubt if these birds on the Marsh ever succeed in bringing off any young; but the large green space is a great attraction, and it is probable that a few stragglers from the country settle down every spring, and that the numbers are thus kept up.

The skylark, starling, and sparrow are the only common resident species. A kestrel hovering above the Marsh is a common sight, and lapwings at certain times of the year are frequent visitors. The resident species are indeed few, but there is no spot near London where anything like so great a variety of waders and water-fowl appear during the autumn and spring migrations, and in severe weather in winter.

There is a great deal of running water in Hackney Marsh, and most of the ground lies between two large currents—the East London Waterworks canal on the west side and the sinuous River Lea on the other side. Midway in its course over the Marsh the river divides, the lesser stream being called Lead Mill Stream ; lower down the currents reunite : thus the land between forms a long, green, flat island. On this island stands the White House, or White House Fishery, close to the bridge over the Lea, a favourite house for anglers in the vanished days when the Lea was a good river to fish in. The anglers have long forsaken it ; but it is a pretty place, standing alone and white on the green level land, surrounded by its few scattered trees, with something of the air about it of a

remote country inn, very restful to London
eyes. It is also a place of memories, but these
are not all of sweet or pleasant things. The
White House was the centre and headquarters
of the Hackney Marsh sportsmen, and the sports
they followed were mostly of that description
which, albeit still permissible, are now generally
regarded as somewhat brutal and blackguardly
in character.

Rabbit coursing, or rabbit worrying, with
terriers; and pigeon, starling, and sparrow
shooting from traps, were the favourite pastimes.
The crowds which gathered to witness these
matches were not nice to see and hear, nor
were they representative of the people of any
London district; they were, in fact, largely composed of the lowest roughs drawn from a population of a million souls—raucous-voiced, lawless,
obscene in their language, filthy in their persons,
and vicious in their habits. Yet you will find
many persons, not of this evil description, who
lament that these doings on the Marsh have been
abolished, so dear is sport of some kind, involving the killing of animals, to the natural man !
Others rejoice at the change. One oldish man,
who said that he had known and loved the

Marsh from boyhood, and had witnessed the sports for very many years, assured me that only since the County Council had taken this open space in hand was it possible for quiet and decent folks to enjoy it. As to the wild bird shooting, he was glad that that too had been done away with; men who spent their Sundays shooting at starlings, larks, and passing pigeons were, he said, a rough lot of blackguards. Two of his anecdotes are worth repeating. One Sunday morning when he was on the Marsh a young sportsman succeeded in bringing down a pigeon which was flying towards London. The bird when picked up was found to have a card attached to its wing—not an unusual occurrence as homing birds were often shot. On the card in this case was written the brief message, 'Mother is dead.' My informant said that it made him sick, but the young sportsman was proud of his achievement.

The other story was of a skylark that made its appearance three summers ago in a vacant piece of ground adjoining Victoria Park. The bird had perhaps escaped from a cage, and was a fine singer, and all day long it could be heard as it flew high above the houses and the park pouring out a continuous torrent of song. It attracted a good deal of attention, and all the Hackney Marsh sportsmen who possessed guns were fired with the desire to shoot it. Every Sunday morning some of them would get into the field to watch their chance to fire at the bird as it rose or returned to the ground; and this shooting went on, and the ' feathered frenzy,' still untouched by a pellet, soared and sung, until cold weather came, when it disappeared.

To return to the White House. This has for the last ninety years been in the possession of a family named Beresford, who have all had a taste for collecting rare birds, and their collection, now split up and distributed among the members of the family, shows that during the last four or five decades Hackney Marsh has been visited by an astonishing variety of wild birds. The chief prize is a cream-coloured courser, the only specimen of this rare straggler from Asia ever obtained in the neighbourhood of London. It was shot on the morning of October 19, 1858, and the story is that a working man came full of excitement to the White House to say that he had just seen a strange bird, looking like a piece of whity-brown paper blowing about on the

Marsh ; whereupon the late Mr. George Beresford took down his gun, went out, and secured the wanderer.

It may be seen on the map of London that Hackney Marsh lies in that broad belt of low wet ground which forms the valley of the Lea, and cuts obliquely through North-east and East London to the Thames at Bugsby's Reach, as that part of the river between Woolwich and the Isle of Dogs is beautifully named. Leyton Marsh, Hackney Marsh, Stratford Marsh, West Ham Abbey Marsh, and Bromley Marsh are all portions of this low strip, over and beyond which London has spread. This marshy valley is not wholly built over ; it contains a great deal of mud and water, and open spaces more or less green ; but on account of the number of factories, gasworks, and noisy industries of various kinds, and of its foul and smoky condition, it is not a home for wild bird life.

Some distance beyond or east of this marshy belt—seven miles east of St. Paul's in the City— there is Wanstead Park, or Wanstead Old Park, and this is the last and outermost public open space and habitation of wild birds belonging

to East London to be described here. Epping
Forest (with Wanstead Flats), although quite
close to Wanstead Park at its nearest end, runs
far into Essex, and lies in a perfectly rural
district. Wanstead Park itself may seem almost
too distant from London to be included here;
but Wanstead village and Snaresbrook are all one,
and Snaresbrook and Leytonstone extend loving
tentacles and clasp each other, and Leytonstone
clasps Leyton, and there is no break in spite of
the mud and water; and the only thing to be
said is that east of the Lea it is Bethnal Green
mitigated or ruralised.

' I was in despair for many days,' some old
traveller has said, relating his adventures in
uninhabited and savage places, ' but at length, to
my great joy, I spied a gibbet, for I then knew
that I was coming to a civilised country.' In
like manner, at Snaresbrook and Leytonstone
many things tell us that we are coming to, and
are practically in, London. But Wanstead
Park itself, and the open country adjoining it,
with its fine old trees, and the River Roding,
when the rains have filled it, winding like a
silver serpent across the green earth, is very
rural and beautiful and refreshing to the sight.

The park (182 acres) is mostly a wood, unlike Highgate, Churchyard Bottom, Wimbledon, or any other wood open to the public near London. It has green spaces and a great deal of water (the lakes and the Roding, which runs through it), and is very charming in its openness, its perfect wildness, and the variety of sylvan scenery contained in it. As might be supposed, this park is peculiarly rich in wild bird life, and among the breeding species may be mentioned mallard and teal, ring-dove and turtle-dove, woodpecker, jay, hawfinch, and nightingale. But the chief attraction is the very large rookery and heronry contained on one of the two large wooded islands. It has sometimes happened when rooks and herons have built on the same trees, or in the same wood, that they have fallen out, and the herons have gone away in disgust to settle elsewhere. At Wanstead no disastrous war has yet taken place, although much quarrelling goes on. The heronry is probably very old, as in 1834 it was described as 'long established and very populous.' The birds subsequently abandoned their old quarters on Heron Island and established their heronry on Lincoln Island, and in

WHITE HOUSE FISHERY, HACKNEY MARSH

WANSTEAD OLD PARK : EARLY SPRING

recent years they appear to have increased, the nests in 1896 numbering fifty or fifty-one, and in 1897 forty-nine.

In conclusion, I wish to suggest that it would be well to make Wanstead Park as far as possible a sanctuary for all wild creatures. A perfect sanctuary it could not very well be made —there are certain creatures which must be kept down by killing. The lake, for instance, is infested by pike—our crocodile, and Nature's chief executioner in these realms. I doubt if the wild duck, teal, little grebe, and moorhen succeed in rearing many young in this most dangerous water. Again, too many jays in this limited space would probably make it very un-comfortable for the other birds. Finally, the place swarms with rats, and as there are no owls, stoats, and weasels to keep them down, man must kill or try to kill them, badly helped by that most miserable of all his servants, the ferret.

But allowing that a perfect sanctuary is not possible, it would be better to do away with the autumn and winter shooting. It is as great a delight to see wild duck, snipe, ring-doves in numbers, and stray waders and water-fowl as

any other feathered creatures ; and it is probable that if guns were not fired here, or not
fired too often, this well-sheltered piece of wood
and water would become the resort in winter of
many persecuted wild birds, and that they would
here lose the excessive wariness which makes
it in most cases so difficult to observe them.

A word must be added concerning the rook-
shooting, which takes place in May, when there
are still a good many young herons in the nests.
At Wanstead I have been seriously told that the
herons are mightily pleased to witness the
annual massacre of their unneighbourly black
neighbours, or their young. My own belief,
after seeing the process, is that the panic of
terror into which the old herons are thrown may
result some day in the entire colony shifting its
quarters into some quieter wood in Essex ; and
that it would be well to adopt some other less
dangerous method of thinning the rooks, if they
are too numerous, which is doubtful.

For the rest, the Corporation are deserving
of nothing but praise for their management of
this invaluable ground. Here is a bit of wild
woodland nature unspoiled by the improving
spirit which makes for prettiness in the Royal

Parks and Kew Gardens and in too many of the
County Council's open spaces. The trees are
not deprived of their lower branches, nor other-
wise mutilated, or cut down because they are
aged or decaying or draped in ivy ; nor are the
wind-chased yellow and russet leaves that give
a characteristic beauty and charm to the winter
woodland here swept up and removed like offensive objects ; nor are the native shrubs and
evergreens rooted up to be replaced by that
always ugly inharmonious exotic, the rhododendron.

CHAPTER XII

SOUTH-EAST LONDON

General survey of South London—South-east London : its most
populous portion—Three small open spaces—Camberwell
New Park — Southwark Park—Kennington Park — Fine
shrubberies—Greenwich Park and Blackheath—A stately
and depressing park—Mutilated trees—The extreme East—
Bostell Woods and Heath—Their peculiar charm—Woolwich
and Plumstead Commons—Hilly Fields—Peckham Rye and
Park—A remonstrance—Nunhead and Camberwell Cemeteries—Dulwich Park—Brockwell Park—The rookery.

SOUTH LONDON, comprising the whole of the
metropolis on the Surrey and Kent side of the
Thames, is not here divided into two districts—
South-east and South-west—merely for con-
venience sake, because it is too large to be dealt
with in one chapter. Considered with reference
to its open spaces and to the physical geography
of this part of the metropolitan area, South
London really comprises two districts differing
somewhat in character.

Taking London to mean the whole of the
area built upon and the outer public open

spaces that touch or abut on streets, or rows of
houses, we find that South London, from east
to west, exceeds North London in length, the
distance from Plumstead and Bostell to Kew and
Old Deer Park being about nineteen miles as the
crow flies. Not, however, as the London crow
flies when travelling up and down river between
these two points, as his custom is : following
the Thames in its windings, his journey each way
would not be a less distance than twenty-seven
to twenty-eight miles. At the eastern end of
South London we find that the open spaces, from
Bostell to Greenwich, lie near the river ; that
from Greenwich the line of open spaces diverges
wide from the river, and, skirting the densely
populated districts, extends southwards through
a hilly country to Brockwell and Sydenham.
On the west side, or the other half of South
London (the South-west district), the open
spaces are, roughly speaking, ranged in a
similar way ; but they are more numerous,
larger, and extend for a much greater distance
along the river—in fact, from Richmond and
Kew to Battersea Park. There the line ends, the
other open spaces being scattered about at a
considerable distance from the river. Thus we

have, between the river on one side and the re-
treating frontier line of open spaces on the other,
a large densely-populated district, containing
few and small breathing-spaces, but not quite
so badly off in this respect as the most crowded
portion of East London.

The Post-Office line dividing the Southern
districts cuts through this populous part of
South London, and has a hilly country on the
left side of the line and a comparatively flat
country on the right or west side. The west
side is the district of large commons ; on the east
side the open spaces are not so many nor, as a
rule, so large, but in many ways they are more
interesting.

All that follows in this chapter will relate
to the open spaces on the east side of the line.

The most densely populated portion of
South-east London lies between Greenwich and
Kennington Oval, a distance of about four
miles and a half. This crowded part contains
about twelve square miles of streets and houses,
and there are in it three open spaces called
'parks,' but quite insignificant in size considering the needs of so vast a population. These

three spaces are Deptford Park, a small space
of 17 acres opened in 1897, Southwark Park,
Kennington Park, and Myatt's Fields; the last
a small open space of fourteen acres, a gift
of Mr. William Minet to the public; formerly
the property of one Myatt, a fruit-grower, and
the first to introduce and cultivate the now
familiar rhubarb in this country.

Southwark Park (63 acres) is the only
comparatively large breathing-place easily
accessible to the working-class population
inhabiting Deptford, Rotherhithe, and Bermondsey.

How great the craving for a breath of fresh
air and the sight of green grass must be in such
a district, when we find that this comparatively
small space has been visited on one day by
upwards of 100,000 persons! An almost incredible number when we consider that less
than half the space contained in the park is
available for the people to walk on, the rest
being taken up by ornamental water, gardens,
shrubberies, enclosures for cricket, &c. The
ground itself is badly shaped, being a long
narrow strip, with conspicuous houses on either
hand, which wall and shut you in and make

the refreshing illusions of openness and distance impossible. Even with a space of fifty or sixty acres, if it be of a proper shape, and the surrounding houses not too high to be hidden by trees, this effect of country-like openness and distance, which gives to a London park its greatest charm and value, can be secured. Again, this being a crowded industrial district full of 'works,' the atmosphere is laden with smoke, and everything that meets the eye, even the leaves and grass, is begrimed with soot. Yet in spite of all these drawbacks Southwark Park is attractive; you admire it as you would a very dirty child with a pretty face. The trees and shrubs have grown well, and there is a lake and island, and ornamental water-fowl. The wild bird life is composed of a multitude of sparrows and a very few blackbirds and thrushes. It is interesting and useful to know that these two species did not settle here themselves, but were introduced by a former superintendent, and have continued to breed for some years.

Kennington Park (19 acres) is less than a third the size of Southwark Park; but though so small and far from other breathing-spaces, in the midst of a populous district, it has a far fresher and prettier aspect than the other. It resembles Highbury Fields more than any other open space, but is better laid out and planted than the miniature North London park. Indeed, Kennington Park is a surprise when first seen, as it actually has larger and better-grown shrubberies than several of the big parks. The shrubberies extend well all around the grounds, and have an exceptionally fine appearance on account of the abundance of holly, the most beautiful of our evergreens. With such a vegetation it is not surprising to find that this small green spot can show a goodly number of songsters. The blackbird, thrush, hedge-sparrow, and robin are here ; but it is hard for these birds to rear their broods, in the case of the robin impossible I should say, on account of the Kennington cats. Here, as in the neighbourhood of the other open spaces in London, the evening cry of ' All out ! ' is to them an invitation to come in.

Two things are needed to make Kennington Park everything that so small a space might and should be : one is the effectual exclusion of the cats, which at present keep down the best songsters ; the other, a small pond or two planted with rushes to attract the moorhens, and

perhaps other species. It may be added that
the cost of making and maintaining a small
pond is less than that of the gardens that
are now being made at Kennington Park,
and that the spectacle of a couple of moorhens
occupied with their domestic affairs in their
little rushy house is infinitely more interesting
than a bed of flowers to those who seek refreshment in our open spaces.

From these small spots of verdure in the
densely-populated portion of South-east London
we must now pass to the larger open spaces in
the outer more rural parts of that extensive
district. The more convenient plan will be to
describe those in the east part first—Greenwich,
Blackheath, and eastwards to Bostell Woods
and Heath ; then, leaving the river, to go the
round of the outer open spaces that lie west of
Woolwich.

Greenwich Park and Blackheath together
contain 452 acres ; but although side by side,
with only a wall and gate to divide them, they
are utterly unlike in character, the so-called
heath being nothing but a large green space
used as a recreation ground, where birds settle

to feed but do not live. Greenwich Park contains 185 acres, inclusive of the enclosed grounds attached to the ranger's lodge, which are now open to the public. But though not more than half the area of Hyde Park, it really strikes one as being very large on account of the hilly broken surface in parts and the large amount of old timber. This park has a curiously aged and somewhat stately appearance, and so long as the back is kept turned on the exceedingly dirty and ugly-looking refreshment building which disgraces it, one cannot fail to be impressed. At the same time I find that this really fine park, which I have known for many years, invariably has a somewhat depressing effect on me. It may be that the historical associations of Greenwich, from the effects of which even those who concern themselves little with the past cannot wholly escape, are partly the cause of the feeling. Its memories are of things dreadful, and magnificent, and some almost ludicrous, but they are all in some degree hateful. After all, perhaps the thoughts of a royal wife-killing ruffian and tyrant, a dying boy king, and a fantastic virgin queen, affect me less than the sight of the old lopped trees. For there are not in all England such melancholy-looking trees as those of Greenwich. You cannot get away from the sight of their sad mutilated condition; and when you walk on and on, this way and that, looking from tree to tree, to find them all lopped off at the same height from the ground, you cannot help being depressed. You are told that they were thus mutilated some twenty to twenty-five years ago to save them from further decay! What should we say of the head physician of some big hospital who should one day issue an order that all patients, indoor and outdoor, should be subjected to the same treatment—that they should be bled and salivated with mercury in the good old way, men, women, and children, whatever their ailments might be? His science would be about on a par with that of the authors of this hideous disfigurement of all the trees in a large park—old and young, decayed and sound, Spanish chestnut, oak, elm, beech, horse-chestnut, every one lopped at the same height from the ground! We have seen in a former chapter what the effect of this measure was on the nobler bird life of the park.

Of all the crows that formerly inhabited

Greenwich, a solitary pair of jackdaws bred until recently in a hollow tree in the ' Wilder ness,' but have lately disappeared. The owls, too, which were seen from time to time down to within about two years ago, appear to have left. The lesser spotted woodpecker and tree-creeper are sometimes seen; nuthatches are not un- common; starlings are very numerous; robins, hedge - sparrows, greenfinches, chaffinches, thrushes, and blackbirds are common In summer several migrants add variety to the bird life, and fieldfares may always be seen in winter. In the gardens and private grounds of Lee, Lewisham, and other neighbouring parishes small birds are more numerous than in the park.

London (streets and houses) extends along or near the river about five miles beyond Greenwich Park. Woolwich and Plumstead now form one continuous populous district, still extending rows of new houses in all available directions, and promising in time to become a new and not very much better Deptford. Plumstead, being mostly new, reminds one of a meaner West Kensington, with its rows on rows of small

houses, gardenless, all exactly alike, as if made
in one mould, and coloured red and yellow to
suit the tenants' fancy.   But at Plumstead,
unlovely and ignoble as it is in appearance, one
has the pleasant thought that at last here, on
this side, one is at the very end of London, that
the country beyond and on either side is, albeit
populous, purely rural.   On the left hand is the
river; on the right of Plumstead is Shooter's
Hill, with green fields, hedges, woods, and preserves, and here some fine views of the surrounding country may be obtained.   Better
still, just beyond Plumstead is the hill which
the builder can never spoil, for here are Bostell
Woods and Heath, the last of London's open
spaces in this direction.

The hill is cut through by a deep road; on
one side are the woods, composed of tall fir-trees
on the broad level top of the hill, and oak,
mixed in places with birch and holly, on the
slopes; on the other side of the road is the
Heath, rough with gorse, bramble, ling, and
bracken, and some pretty patches of birch wood.
From this open part there are noble views of the
Kent and Essex marshes, the river with its steely
bright sinuous band dividing the counties.

Woods and heath together have an area of 132 acres ; but owing to the large horizon, the broken surface, and the wild and varied character of the woodland scenery, the space seems practically unlimited : the sense of freedom, which gives Hampstead Heath its principal charm and tonic value, may be here experienced in even a greater degree than at that favourite resort. To the dwellers in the north, west, and south-west of London this wild spot is little known. From Paddington or Victoria you can journey to the end of Surrey and to Hampshire more quickly and with greater comfort than to Bostell Woods. To the very large and increasing working population of Woolwich and Plumstead this space is of incalculable value, and they delight in it. But this is a busy people, and on most working days, especially in the late autumn, winter, and early spring months, the visitor will often find himself out of sight and sound of human beings ; nor could the lover of nature and of contemplation wish for a better place in which to roam about. Small woodland birds are in great variety. Quietly moving about or seated under the trees, you hear the delicate songs and various airy lisping and tinkling

sounds of tits of several species, of wren, tree-
creeper, goldcrest, nuthatch, lesser spotted
woodpecker, robin, greenfinch and chaffinch,
and in winter the siskin and redpole. Listening to this fairy-like musical prattle, or attend-
ing to your own thoughts, there is but one
thing, one sound, to break the illusion of
remoteness from the toiling crowded world of
London—the report at intervals of a big gun
from the Arsenal, three miles away. Too far
for the jarring and shrieking sounds of machinery
and the noisy toil of some sixteen to eighteen
thousand men perpetually engaged in the manu-
facture of arms to reach the woods ; but the dull,
thunderous roar of the big gun travels over wide
leagues of country ; and the hermit, startled out
of his meditations, is apt to wish with the poet
that the old god of war himself was dead, and
rotting on his iron hills ; or else that he would
make his hostile preparations with less noise.

At the end of day, windless after wind, or
with a clear sky after rain, when the guns
have ceased to boom, the woods are at their
best. Then the birds are most vocal, their
voices purer, more spiritual, than at other
times. Then the level sun, that flatters all

BOSTELL HEATH AND WOOD

THE ROOKERY, BROCKWELL PARK

things, fills the dim interior with a mystic light, a strange glory; and the oaks, green with moss, are pillars of emerald, and the tall red-barked fir-trees are pillars of fire.

Some reader, remembering the exceeding foulness of London itself, and the polluting cloud which it casts wide over the country, to this side or that according as the wind blows, may imagine that no place in touch with the East-end of the metropolis can be quite so fresh as I have painted Bostell. But Nature's self-purifying power is very great. Those who are well acquainted with outer London, within a radius of, say, ten miles of Charing Cross, must know spots as fresh and unsullied as you would find in the remote Quantocks; secluded bits of woodland where you can spend hours out of sight and sound of human life, forgetting London and the things that concern London, or by means of the mind's magic changing them into something in harmony with your own mood and wholly your own:

> Annihilating all that's made
> To a green thought in a green shade.

Bostell Woods is a favourite haunt of birds'-nesting boys and youths in summer, and as it is quite impossible to keep an eye on their doings, very few of the larger and rarer species are able to breed there; but in the adjoining wooded grounds, belonging to Christ's Hospital, the jay, magpie, white owl and brown owl still breed, and the nightingale is common in summer.

Not far from Bostell we have the Plumstead and Woolwich Commons, together an area of about 450 acres; but as these spaces are used solely as recreation grounds, and are not attractive to birds, it is not necessary to describe them. West and south-west of Greenwich, in that rural portion of the South-east district through which our way now lies, the first open space we come to is the Hilly Fields (45 acres) at Brockley; a green hill with fine views from the summit, .but not a habitation of birds. A little farther on, with Nunhead Cemetery between, lies Peckham Rye and Peckham Rye Park (113 acres). The Rye, or common, is a wedge-shaped piece of ground used for recreation, and consequently not a place where birds are found. From the

narrow end of the ground a very attractive
prospect lies before the sight : the green wide
space of the Rye is seen to be bounded by a
wood (the park), and beyond the wood are
green hills—Furze Hill, and One Tree, or Oak
of Honor, Hill. The effect of distance is produced by the trees and hills, and the scene is,
for this part of London, strikingly rural. The
park at the broad extremity of the Rye, I
have said, has the appearance of a wood ; and
it is or was a wood, or the well-preserved fragment of one, as perfect a transcript of wild
nature as could be found within four miles of
Charing Cross. This park was acquired for the
public in 1891, and as the wildest and best portion was enclosed with an iron fence to keep
the public out, some of us cherished the hope
that the County Council meant to preserve it in
the exact condition in which they received it.
There the self-planted and never mutilated trees
flourished in beautiful disorder, their lower
boughs mingling with the spreading luxuriant
brambles ; and tree, bramble, and ivy were
one with the wild grasses and woodland
blossoms among them. If, as tradition tells,
King John hunted the wild stag at Peckham, he

could not have seen a fresher, lovelier bit of nature than this. But, alas ! the gardeners, who had all the rest of the grounds to prettify and vulgarise and work their will on, could not keep their hands off this precious spot ; for some time past they have been cutting away the wild growths, and digging and planting, until they have well nigh spoiled it.

There is no doubt that a vast majority of the inhabitants of London, whose only glimpses of nature can be had in the public parks, prefer that that nature should be as little spoiled as possible ; that there should be something of wildness in it, of Nature's own negligence. It is infinitely more to them than that excessive smoothness and artificiality of which we see so much. To exhibit flower-beds to those who crave for nature is like placing a dish of Turkish Delight before a hungry man : a bramble-bush, a bunch of nettles, would suit him better. And this universal feeling and perpetual want of the Londoner should be more considered by those who have charge of our open spaces.

Small birds are abundant in Peckham Park, but there is no large species except the now almost universal wood-pigeon. A few rooks, in 1895, and again in 1896, tried to establish a rookery here, but have now gone away. The resident songsters are the thrush, blackbird, robin, dunnock, wren, tits, chaffinch, greenfinch, and starling. Among the blackbirds there are, at the time of writing this chapter, two white individuals.

Close to Peckham Rye and Park there are two large cemeteries—Nunhead on one side and Camberwell Cemetery on the other. Both are on high ground; the first (40 acres) is an extremely pretty spot, and has the finest trees to be seen in any metropolitan burying-ground. From the highest part of the ground an extensive and charming view may be had of the comparatively rural district on the south side. Small birds, especially in the winter months, are numerous in this cemetery, and it is pretty to see the starlings in flocks, chaffinches, robins, and other small birds sitting on the gravestones.

Camberwell Cemetery is smaller and newer, and has but few trees, but is on even higher ground, as it occupies a slope of the hill above the park. If there is any metropolitan

burying-ground where dead Londoners find
a post-mortem existence tolerable, it must, I
imagine, be on this spot; since by perching or
sitting on their own tombstones they may enjoy a wide view of South-east London—a pleasant prospect of mixed town and country, of
houses and trees, and tall church spires, and
green slopes of distant hills.

It is to be hoped that when this horrible
business of burying our dead in London is
brought to an end, Nunhead and Camberwell
Cemeteries will be made one large open space
with Peckham Rye and Park.

A mile from the Rye is Dulwich Park
(72 acres); it is laid out more as a garden
than a park, and may be said to be one of
the prettiest and least interesting of the metropolitan open spaces. I mean ' prettiest ' in the
sense in which gardeners and women use the
word. It lies in the midst of one of the most
rural portions of South-east London, having on
all sides large private gardens, park-like grounds,
and woods. The bird life in this part is
abundant, including in summer the blackcap,
garden-warbler, willow-wren, wood-wren, redstart, pied wagtail, tree pipit, and cuckoo. The

large birds commonly seen are the rook, carrion
crow, daw, and wood-pigeon. The park itself,
being so much more artificial than the adjacent
grounds, has comparatively few birds.

A mile west of Dulwich Park, touching the
line dividing the South-east and South-west
districts, is Brockwell Park (78 acres). Like
Clissold and Ravenscourt, this is one of the old
private parks of London, with a manor house in
it, now used as a refreshment house. It is very
open, a beautiful green hill, from which there
are extensive and some very charming views.
Knight's Hill, not yet built upon, is close by.
The elm-trees scattered all about the park are
large and well grown, and have a healthy look.
On one part of the ground is a walled-round
delightful old garden—half orchard—the only
garden containing fruit-trees, roses, and old-
fashioned herbs and flowers in any open space
in London. Another great attraction is—I fear
we shall before long have to say *was*—the
rookery. Six years ago it was the most populous rookery in or near London, and extended
over the entire park, there being few or no large
trees without nests ; but when the park was

opened to the public, in 1891, the birds went away, all excepting those that occupied nests on the large trees at the main gate, which is within a few yards of Herne Hill station. They were evidently so used to the noise of the trains and traffic, and to the sight of people in the thoroughfare on which they looked down, that the opening of the park did not disturb them. Nevertheless this remnant of the old rookery is becoming less populous each year. In the summer of 1896 I counted thirty-five occupied nests ; in 1897 there were only twenty nests. Just now—February 1898—eight or ten pairs of birds are engaged in repairing the old nests.

It is very pleasant to find that here, at all events, very little (I cannot say nothing) has so far been done to spoil the natural character and charm of this park—one of the finest of London's open spaces.

CHAPTER XIII

SOUTH-WEST LONDON

IN the foregoing chapters the arbitrary lines dividing the London postal districts have not been always strictly kept to. Thus, the Green Park and St. James's Park, which are in the South-west, were included in the West district. simply because the central parks, with Holland Park, form one group, or rather one chain of open spaces. In treating of the South-west

district it will again be found convenient
to disregard the line at some points, since, besides excluding the two parks just named, I
propose to include Kew Gardens, Richmond
Park, and Wimbledon Common—large spaces
which lie for the most part outside of the Post-
Office boundary.   These spaces do nevertheless
form an integral part of London as it has been
defined for the purposes of this book: they
belong to the South-west district in the same
way that Hampstead Heath does to the North-
west, Hackney Marsh and Wanstead Old Park
to the East, Plumstead and Bostell to the South-
east.   All these open spaces *touch* London,
although they are not entirely cut off from the
country.   Again, for the same reason which
made me exclude Epping Forest, Ham Common,
&c., from the East district, I now exclude
Hampton Court Park and Bushey Park from the
South-west.   It might be said that Richmond
Park is not less rural than Bushey Park, or even
than Epping Forest; that with regard to their
wild bird life all these big open spaces on the
borders of London are in the same category;
but the line must be drawn somewhere, and
having made my rule I must keep to it.   Doubt-

ess before many years the tide of buildings will lave completely encircled and flowed beyond the outermost open spaces described in this and the preceding chapters.

Within these limits we find that the South-west district, besides being the least densely populated portion of London, is immeasurably better off in open spaces than any other. There is, in fact, no comparison. The following is a very rough statement of the amount of space open to the public in each of the big districts, omitting the cemeteries, and all gardens, squares, greens, recreation grounds, and all other open spaces of less than ten acres in size. West London, *including* Green Park and St. James's Park, has about 1,500 acres. North London (North-west and North districts), which has two very large spaces in Regent's Park and Hampstead Heath, has about 1,300 acres. East London, excluding Epping Forest, Wanstead Flats, and Ham Common, has less than 1,000 acres. South-east London, 1,500 to 1,600 acres. South-west London has about 7,500 acres, or 2,200 acres more than all the other districts together. This does not include Old Deer Park, which is not open to the public. If we include Green,

St. James's, Bushey, and Hampton Court Parks,
the South-west district would then have about
8,650 acres in large open spaces. All the rest
of London, with the whole vast space of Epping
Forest thrown in, would have 7,500, or 1,150
acres less than the South-west district.

The large open spaces of South-west London,
although more scattered about than is the case
in other metropolitan districts, do nevertheless
form more or less well-defined groups. Battersea Park is an exception : it is the only open
space in this district which has, so to speak,
been entirely remade, the digging and planting,
which have been so vigorously going on for
several years past, having quite obliterated its
original character. Coming to speak of the
open spaces in detail, I propose first to describe
this made park; to go next to the large
commons south of Battersea—Clapham, Wandsworth, Tooting, and Streatham ; then, returning
to the river-side, to describe Bishop's Park,
Fulham, and its near neighbour, Barnes Common ; and, finally, to go on to the large spaces
at Kew, Putney, Wimbledon, and Richmond.

Battersea Park (198 acres), formerly a marsh,

has within the last few years been transformed into the most popular open-air resort in the metropolis. The attempt to please everybody usually ends in pleasing nobody; at Battersea the dangerous experiment has been tried with success; for no person would be so unreasonable as to look for that peculiar charm of wildness, which still lingers in Bostell Heath and Wimbledon Common, in a garden planted in a marsh close to the heart of London. The ground has certainly been made the most of: the flat surface has been thrown into mounds, dells, and other inequalities; there are gardens and rockeries, large well-grown trees of many kinds, magnificent shrubberies, and, best of all, a pretty winding lake, with an area of about 16 acres, and large well-wooded islands on it. Besides the attraction which the beautiful grounds, the variety of plants and of ornamental water-fowl and other animals have for people generally, crowds are drawn to this spot by the facilities afforded for recreations of various kinds— boating, cycling, cricket, tennis, &c. This popularity of Battersea is interesting to us incidentally when considering its wild bird life, for it might be supposed that the number of people and the incessant noise would drive away the shyer species, and that the birds would be few. This is not the case : the wild bird life is actually far more abundant and varied than in any other inner London park. Mere numbers and noise of people appear to have little effect on birds so long as they are protected.

Battersea Park has a good position to attract birds passing through or wandering about London, as these are apt to follow the river ; and it also has the advantage of being near the central parks, which, as we have seen, serve as a kind of highway by which birds come into London from the west side. In the park itself the lake and wooded islands, and extensive shrubberies with dense masses of evergreen, tempt them to build. But it must also be said, in justice, that the superintendent of this park fully appreciates the value of the birds, and takes every pains to encourage and protect them. A few years ago, when he came to Battersea, there were about a dozen blackbirds ; now as many as forty have been counted feeding in the early morning on one lawn ; and in spring and summer, at about four o'clock every morning, there is such a concert of thrushes and black-

birds, with many other bright voices, as would
be hard to match in any purely rural district.
It is interesting to know that the wren, which is
dying out in other London parks, has steadily
increased at Battersea, and is now quite
common. Robins and hedge-sparrows are also
more numerous than in our other open spaces.
A number of migrants are attracted to this spot
every summer ; of these the pied wagtail, lesser
whitethroat, reed-warbler, and cuckoo bred
last season. The larger birds are the wood-
pigeon, moorhen, dabchick, and to these the
carrion crow may now be added as a breeding
species.

Clapham Common (220 acres) is the nearest
to central London of that large, loose group of
commons distinctive of the South-west district,
its distance from Battersea being a little over a
mile, and from Charing Cross about three miles
and a half. Like Hackney Downs, it is a grassy
space, but flatter, and having the appearance of
a piece of ground not yet built upon it may be
described as the least interesting open space in
the metropolis. To the smoke and dust breathing, close-crowded inhabitants of Bethnal Green,

which is not green nor of any other colour
found in nature, this expanse of grass, if they
had it within reach, would be an unspeakable
boon, and seem to their weary eyes like a field
in paradise. But Clapham is not over-crowded;
it is a place of gardens full of fluttering leaves,
and the exceeding monotony of its open space,
set round with conspicuous houses, must cause
those who live near it to sigh at the thought of
its old vanished aspect when the small boy
Thomas Babington Macaulay roamed over its
broken surface, among its delightful poplar
groves and furze and bramble bushes, or hid
himself in its grass-grown gravel-pits, the world
forgetting, by his nurse forgot. These grateful
inequalities and roughnesses have been smoothed
over, and the ancient vegetation swept away
like dead autumn leaves from the velvet lawns
and gravel walks of a trim suburban villa.
When this change was effected I do not know:
probably a good while back. To the Clapham-
ites of the past the furze must have seemed
an unregenerate bush, and the bramble something worse, since its recurved thorns would
remind them of an exceedingly objectionable
person's finger-nails. As for the yellowhammer,

that too gaily apparelled idle singer, who painted his eggs with so strange a paint, it must indeed have been a relief to get rid of him.

At present Clapham Common is no place for birds.

Wandsworth Common (183 acres) is a very long strip of ground, unfortunately very narrow, with long monotonous rows of red brick houses, hideous in their uniformity, at its sides. Here there is no attempt at disguise, no illusion of distance, no effect of openness left: the cheap speculative builder has been permitted to spoil it all. A railway line which cuts very nearly through the whole length of the common still further detracts from its value as a breathing-space. The broadest part of the ground at its western extremity has a good deal of furze growing on it, and here the common joins an extensive piece of ground, park-like in character, on which stands an extremely picturesque old red brick house. When this green space is built upon Wandsworth will lose the little that remains of its ancient beauty and freshness.

Among the small birds still to be found here

is the yellowhammer, and it strikes one as very curious to hear his song in such a place. Why does he stay? Is he tempted by the little bit of bread and no cheese which satisfies his modest wants—the small fragments dropped by the numberless children that play among the bushes after school hours? The yellowhammer does not colonise with us; he goes and returns not, and this is now the last spot in the metropolis within four miles and a half of Charing Cross where he may still be found. He was cradled on the common, and does not know that there are places on the earth where the furze-bushes are unblackened by smoke, where at intervals of a few minutes the earth is not shaken by trains that rush thundering and shrieking, as if demented, into or out of Clapham Junction.

I fear the yellowhammer will not long remain in such a pandemonium. The people of Wandsworth are hardly deserving of such a bird.

Tooting Common is the general name for two commons — Tooting Bec and Tooting Graveney, 144 and 66 acres respectively. A public road divides them, but they form really one area. Tooting Bec has a fair amount of gorse and bramble bushes scattered about, and a good many old trees, mostly oak. The number of old trees gives this space something of a park-like appearance, but it is not exhilarating; on the contrary, its effect on the mind is rather depressing, on account of the perfect flatness of the ground and the sadly decayed and smoke-blackened condition of the trees. An 'improvement' of the late Metropolitan Board of Works was the planting of a very long and very straight avenue of fast-growing black poplars, and this belt of weed-like ungraceful trees, out of keeping with everything, has made Tooting Bec positively ugly.

Another improvement has been introduced by the County Council; this is the usual small pond and the usual couple of big swans. The rage for putting these huge birds in numberless small ponds and miniature lakes can only proceed from a singular want of imagination on the part of the park gardeners and park decorators employed by the Council; or we might suppose that the Council have purchased a big job lot of swans, which they are anxious to distribute about London. These dreary little ponds might easily be made exceedingly interesting, if planted round with willows and rushes and stocked with a few of the smaller pretty ornamental water-fowl in place of their present big unsuitable occupants.

Tooting Graveney has a fresher, wilder aspect, and is a pleasanter place than its sister common. Its surroundings, too, are far more rural, as it has for neighbours Streatham Park and the wide green spaces of Furze Down and Totterdown Fields. Tooting Graveney itself is in the condition of the old Clapham Common as Macaulay knew it in his boyhood. Its surface is rough with grass-grown mounds, old gravel-pits, and excavations, and it is grown over with bushes of furze, bramble, and brier, and with scattered birch-trees and old dwarf hawthorns, looking very pretty. Wild birds are numerous, although probably few are able to rear any young on the common. The misselthrush, now very rare in London, breeds in private grounds close by.

Streatham Common (66 acres) is the least as well as the outermost of the group of large commons; it is but half the size of Clapham

Common. But though so much smaller than the others, it is the most interesting, owing to the hilly nature of the ground and to the fine prospect to be had of the country beyond. It

NIGHTINGALE ON ITS NEST

forms a rather long strip, and from the highest part at the upper end the vision ranges over the beautifully wooded and hilly Surrey country to and beyond Epsom. This upper end of the common is extremely pretty, overgrown with furze and bramble bushes, and pleasantly shaded with trees at one side. Birds when breeding

cannot be protected on the common; the wild
bird life is nevertheless abundant and varied, on
account of the large private grounds adjoining.
It is pleasant to sit here on a spring or summer
day and watch the jays that come to the trees
overhead; like other London jays and the
London fieldfares, they are strangely tame compared with these birds in the country.   Out in
the sunshine the skylark mounts up singing;
and here, too, may be heard the nightingale.
He does not merely make a short stay on his
arrival in spring, as at some other spots in
the suburbs, but remains to breed.   Yet here
we are only six and a half miles from Charing
Cross.   It is still more surprising to find the
magpie at Streatham, in the wooded grounds
which join the common.   Rooks are numerous
at Streatham, and their rookery close to
Streatham Common station is a singularly interesting one.   It is on an avenue of tall elms
which formerly stood on open grass-land.   A
few years ago this land was built over, rows of
houses being erected on each side of and
parallel with the avenue, which now stands
in the back gardens or yards, with the back
windows of the houses looking on it.   But

in spite of all these changes, and the large
human population gathered round them, the
birds have stuck to their rookery ; and last
summer (1897) there were about thirty inhabited
nests.

From Streatham we go back to the river, to
a point about a mile and a half west of Wandsworth Common, to Fulham Palace grounds on
the Middlesex side, and the open spaces at
Barnes on the Surrey side.

Bishop's Park, Fulham, of which about 12
acres are free to the public, is one of London's
rare beauty-spots. A considerable portion of
the palace grounds is within the moat, and the
moat, the noble old trees, and wide green
spaces, form an appropriate setting to the
ancient stately Bishop's Palace. The lamentable
mistake has been made of placing this open space
in the control of the Fulham Vestry ; and, as might
have been expected, they have been improving
it in accordance with the æsthetic ideas of the
ordinary suburban tradesman, by cutting down
the old trees, planting rows of evergreens to hide
the beautiful inner grounds from view, and by
erecting cast-iron painted fountains, shelters, and

other architectural freaks of a similar character.
That the inhabitants of Fulham can see unmoved
this vulgarisation of so noble and beautiful a
remnant of the past—the spot in London which
recalls the moated Bishop's Palace at Wells—
is really astonishing.

To the bird-lover as well as to the student
of history this is a place of memories, for here
in the time of Henry VIII. spoonbills and herons
built their nests on the old trees in the bishop's
grounds. At the present time there are some
sweet songsters—thrush, blackbird, robin, dunnock, wren, chaffinch, and a few summer visitants. Here, too, we find the wood-pigeon, but
not the 'ecclesiastical daw' or other distinguished species, and, strange to say, no moat-
hen in the large old moat. How much more
interesting this water would be, with its grass-
grown banks and ancient shade-giving trees,
if it had a few feathered inhabitants ! Simply
by lowering the banks at a few points and
planting some reeds and rushes, it would quickly
attract those two very common and always
interesting London species, the moorhen and the
little grebe. The sedge-warbler, too, would perhaps come in time.

I have been informed that London Bishops care for none of these things.

Looking across the river from Fulham Palace grounds, an extensive well-wooded space is seen on the south bank ; this is Barn Elms Park, now occupied by the Ranelagh Sporting Club. It is one of the best private parks in London, with fine old elm-trees and a lake, and would be a paradise of wild birds but for the shooting which goes on there and scares them away.

Close to Barn Elms is Barnes Common (100 acres), a pleasant open heath, not all flat, grown with heather, and dotted with furze and bramble bushes and a few trees. One of its attractions is Beverley Brook, which rises near Malden, about eight miles away, and flows by Coombe Woods, Wimbledon, through Richmond Park, and, finally, by Barnes Common to the Thames : the brook and a very pretty green meadow separate the common from Barn Elms Park.

The London and South-Western Railway Company have been allowed to appropriate a portion of this open space ; but that indeed seems a very small matter when we find that the parishes of Barnes and Putney have established two cemeteries on the common, using a good many of its scanty 100 acres for the purpose. What would be said if the Government were to allow two cemeteries for the accommodation of the parishes of Kensington and Paddington to be made in the middle of Kensington Gardens? I fail to see that it is less an outrage to have turned a portion of Barnes Common into hideous walled round Golgothas, with mortuary chapels, the ground studded with grave-stones and filled with putrefying corpses. It is devoutly to be hoped that before very long the people of London will make the discovery that it rests with themselves whether their house shall be put in order or not; and when that time comes that these horrible forests of grave-stones and monuments to the dead will be brushed away, and that such bodies as the Barnes Conservators and the Fulham Vestry will for ever be deprived of the powers they so lamentably misuse.

It would be difficult for any bird, big or little, to rear its young on a space so unprotected as this common; many birds, however, come to it, attracted by its open heath-like character. Here the skylark and yellowhammer may be heard, as well as the common resident songsters found in other open spaces. The carrion crow is a constant visitor, and very tame, knowing that he is safe. Beverley Brook has no aquatic birds in it, but it would be easy to make a small rushy sanctuary in the marshy borders, protected from mischievous persons, for the moorhen, sedge-warbler, and other species. I have seen a small boy with an earthworm at the end of a piece of thread pull out thirty to forty minnows in as many minutes. Little grebes and kingfishers would not want for food in such a place.

South and west of Barnes Common, London, as we progress, becomes increasingly rural, with large private park-like grounds, until we arrive at the open spaces of Putney Heath, Lower Putney Common, and Wimbledon Common, which together form an area of 1,412 acres, or nearly three times as large as Hampstead Heath. It seems only appropriate that the most rural portion of the most rural district in London should have so large an open space, and that in character this space should be wilder and more refreshing to the spirit than any other in the

metropolis.   It has the further advantage (from
the point of view of the residents) of not being
too easy of access to the mass of the people.
This makes it ' select,' a semi-private recreation
ground for the residents, and a ' Happy Hampstead ' to a limited number of cockneys of a
superior kind.   Here the fascinating game of
golf, excluded from other public spaces, may
be practised ; and the golfer, arrayed like the
poppies of the cornfield and visible at a vast
distance, strolls leisurely about as his manner
is, or stands motionless to watch the far flight
of his small ball, which will kill no one and hit
no one, since strangers moving about on the
grounds are actually fewer than would be seen
on the links at Hayling, or even Minehead.

It is a solitary place, and its solitariness is
its principal charm.   A wide open heath, with
some pretty patches of birch wood, stretches of
brown heather, dotted in places with furze-
bushes like little black islands ; but on that
part which is called Putney Heath furze and
bramble and brier grow thick and luxuriant.
One may look far in some directions and see
no houses nor other sign of human occupancy
to spoil the effect of seclusion and wildness.

Over all is the vast void sky and the rapturous music of the skylark.

At Wimbledon one has the idea of being at a considerable elevation ; the highest point is really only 300 feet above the sea level, but it is set in a deep depression, and from some points the sight may range as far as the hills about Guildford and Godalming. There are persons of sensitive olfactories who affirm that when the wind blows from the south coast they can smell the sea-salt in it.

But Wimbledon is not all open heath and common ; it has also an extensive wood, delightfully wild, the only large birch wood near the metropolis. The missel-thrush, nuthatch, and tree-creeper breed here, and the jay is common and tame ; I have seen as many as six together. In this wood a finer concert of nightingales may be heard in summer than at any other place near London. In winter fieldfares and pewits are often seen. Carrion crows from Coombe Woods and other breeding-places in the neighbourhood are constantly seen on the common in pairs and small parties, and are strangely familiar. Rooks, too, are extremely abundant. Richmond Park is their roosting-place in winter, and there are numerous rookeries, large and small, in the neighbourhood —at Sheen Gate, at various points along the Kingston road, at Norbiton and Kingston, on the estate of the late Madame Lyne Stevens, at Coombe Woods, and at Wimbledon itself, in some large elms growing at the side of the High Street on Sir Henry Peek's property. Concerning this rookery there is an interesting fact to relate. About six years ago the experiment of shooting the young rooks was tried, with the very best intentions, the rookery being greatly prized. But these rooks were not accustomed to be thinned down (for their own good) every summer, and they forsook the trees. Everything was then done to entice them back; artificial nests were constantly kept on the tree-tops, and in winter food in abundance was placed for the birds; but though they came readily enough to regale on bread and scraps they refused to settle until last spring (1897), when they returned in a body and rebuilt the rookery.

This book is mainly about birds, but I cannot help mentioning the fact that in the wood at Wimbledon that rare and interesting mammal, the badger, found at only one other spot on the borders of London, is permitted to spend his hermit life in peace.

> Here, in solitude and shade,
> Shambling, shuffling plantigrade,
> Be thy courses undismayed.

It may seem almost absurd in writing of a London wild animal to quote from Bret Harte's ode to the great grizzly in the Western wilderness! Nevertheless Wimbledon may be proud to possess even the poor little quaint timid badger —cousin, a million times removed, to the mighty bear, the truculent coward, as the poet says, with tiger claws on baby feet, who has a giant's strength and is satisfied to prey on wasps' nests.

Recently, on one of the largest estates in England, in a part of the country where the badger is now all but extinct, it was reported at the big house that a pair of these animals had established themselves in the forest, which, it may be mentioned, is very large—about eighteen miles round. A grand campaign was at once organised, and a large number of men and boys, armed with guns, spades, hatchets, pitchforks, and bludgeons, and followed by many dogs, went out to the attack. Arrived at the den, at the roots of a giant beech-tree, they set to work to dig the animals out. It was a huge task, but there were many to help, and in the end the badgers were found, old and young together, and killed.

Let us imagine that when this business was proceeding with tremendous excitement and noise of shouting men and barking dogs, some person buried at that spot in old Palæo-lithic times had been raised up to view the spectacle ; that it had been explained to him that these hunters were his own remote de-scendants ; that one of them was a mighty nobleman, a kind of chief or king, whose possessions extended on every side as far as the eye could see ; that the others were his followers who served and obeyed him ; and that they were all engaged in hunting and killing the last badger, the most terrible wild beast left in the land ! I think that the old hunter, who, with his rude stone-headed spear had fought with and overcome even mightier beasts than the grizzly bear, would have emitted a strange and perhaps terrifying sound, a burst of primitive laughter very shrill and prolonged, resembling the neigh of a wild horse, or perhaps deep, from a deep chest, like the baying of a bloodhound.

Richmond Park (2,470 acres) both in its vast extent and character is unlike any other metropolitan open space. The noblest of the breathing-spaces on our borders, it is also the most accessible, and more or less well known to tens of thousands of persons ; but it is probably intimately known only to a few. Speaking for myself, I can say that after having visited it occasionally for years, sometimes to spend a whole day in it, sometimes to get lost in it, both in fine and foggy weather, I do not know it so well as other large open spaces which have not been visited more often. Any person well acquainted with the country would probably find it easy at a moment's notice to name half a dozen parks which have pleased him better than this one, on account of a certain monotony in the scenery of Richmond, but in size it would surpass most or all of them. So large is it that half a dozen such London parks as Clissold, Waterlow, and Ravenscourt might easily be hidden in one corner of it, where it would not be easy to find them. There are roads running in various directions, and on most days many persons may be seen on them, driving, riding, cycling, and walking; yet they all may be got away from, and long hours spent out of sight and hearing of human beings, in the most perfect solitude. This is the greatest attraction of Richmond Park, and its best virtue. Strange to say, this very quietude and solitariness produce a disturbing effect on many Londoners. Alas for those who have so long existed apart from Nature as to have become wholly estranged, who are troubled in mind at her silence and austerity! To others this green desert is London's best possession, a sacred place where those who have lost their strength may find it again, and those who are distempered may recover their health.

The largeness and quietness of Richmond, its old oak woods, water, and wide open spaces, and its proximity to the river, have given it not only an abundant but a nobler wild bird life than is found at any other point so near to the centre of the metropolis. Here all the best songsters, including the nightingale, may be heard. Wild duck and teal and a few other water birds, rear their young in the ponds. Our

two most beautiful woodland birds, the green
woodpecker and the jay, are common. Rooks
are numerous, especially in winter, when they
congregate to roost. Here, too, you may hear
the carrion crow's 'voice of care.' Jackdaws
are certainly more plentiful than anywhere
within one hundred miles of London. One day
I counted fifty in a flock, and saw them settle
on the trees; then going a little distance on I
saw another flock numbering about forty, and
beyond this lot from another wood sounded
the clamour of a third flock. Even then I had
probably not seen *all* the Richmond daws;
perhaps not more than half the entire number,
for I was assured by a keeper that there were
' millions.' He was a very tall white-haired old
man with aquiline features and dark fierce eyes,
and therefore must have known what he was
talking about.

Best of all are the herons that breed in the
park, and appear to be increasing. One fine
evening in February last I counted twenty
together at Sidmouth Wood. A multitude of
rooks and daws had settled on the tree-tops
where the herons were; but after a few minutes
they rose up with a great noise, and were

followed by the herons, who mounted high
above the black cawing crowd, looking very
large and majestic against the pale clear sky.
It was the finest spectacle in wild bird life I had
ever seen so close to London.

It is a great thing for Richmond to have the
heron, which is no longer common; and now
that the kite, buzzard, and raven have been lost,
it is the only large soaring inland species which,
once seen, appears as an indispensable part of
the landscape. Take it away, and the large
comparatively wild nature loses half its charm.

In a former chapter I have endeavoured to
show how great the æsthetic value of the daw is
to our cathedrals. The old dead builders of
these great temples owe perhaps as much to
this bird as to the softening and harmonising
effects of time and weather. Again, every one
must feel that the effect of sublimity produced
on us by our boldest cliffs is greatly enhanced
by the sea-fowl, soaring along the precipitous
face of the rocks, and peopling their ledges, tier
above tier of birds, the highest, seen from below,
appearing as mere white specks. A similar
effect is produced by large soaring birds on any
inland landscape; the horizon is widened and

the sky lifted to an immeasurable height. Some such idea as this, of the indescribable charm of the large soaring bird, of its value to the artistic eye in producing the effect of distance and vastness in nature, was probably in our late lost artist-poet's mind when he painted the following exquisite word-picture :—

High up and light are the clouds ; and though the
     swallows flit
So high above the sunlit earth, they are well a part
     of it ;
And so though high over them are the wings of the
     wandering hern,
In measureless depths above him doth the fair sky
     quiver and burn.

Speaking for myself, without the ' wandering hern,' or buzzard, or other large soaring species, the sky does not impress me with its height and vastness ; and without the sea-fowl the most tremendous sea-fronting cliff is a wall which may be any height ; and the noblest cathedral without any jackdaws soaring and gamboling about its towers is apt to seem little more than a great barn, or a Dissenting chapel on a gigantic scale.

Kew Gardens, with the adjoining spaces of Old Deer Park and the Queen's Private Grounds,

comprising an area of about 600 acres, with a
river frontage of over two miles, is in even
closer touch with London than its near neighbour, Richmond Park. From the heart of the
city two principal thoroughfares run west, and,
uniting on the farther side of Hammersmith,
extend with few breaks in the walls of brick
and glass on either side to Kew Bridge. The
distance from the Mansion House to the bridge
is about ten miles, and the few remaining gaps
in the westernmost portion of this long busy
way are now rapidly being filled up. What
was formerly the village of Kew is now an
integral part of London the Monotonous, in
appearance just like other suburbs—Wormwood
Scrubs, Kilburn, Muswell Hill, Green Lanes,
Dulwich, and Norwood.

Kew Gardens (251 acres) is, or until very
recently was, one of the three or four spots on
the borders of the metropolis most favoured by
the birds. They were attracted to it by its
large size, the woodland character of most of
the ground, and its unrivalled position on the
river in the immediate vicinity of several other
extensive open spaces. The breeding place of
most of the birds was in the Queen's Private

Grounds, a wedge of land between the Gardens and Old Deer Park, a wilderness and perfect sanctuary for all wild creatures. In this green wooded spot and the adjoining gardens the following species have bred annually: misselthrush, throstle, blackbird, redstart, robin, nightingale, whitethroat, lesser whitethroat, blackcap, garden - warbler, chiffchaff, willow - wren, wood-wren, sedge-warbler, dunnock, wren, great, coal, blue, and long-tailed tits, nuthatch, tree-creeper, pied wagtail, tree-pipit, spotted flycatcher, swallow, house-martin, greenfinch, common sparrow, chaffinch, starling, jay, crow, swift, green and lesser woodpecker, wryneck, cuckoo, pheasant, partridge, wood-pigeon, moorhen, dabchick—in all forty-three species. Besides these there is good reason to believe that the following six species have been breeders in the Queen's grounds during recent years: goldcrest, marsh tit, goldfinch, hawfinch, bullfinch, and magpie.

This list will prove useful to London naturalists in the near future, as many changes in the bird life of Kew may shortly be looked for. With the opening of the Queen's grounds the partridge and pheasant will cease to breed there;

the crow is not now allowed to build in the
gardens ; the nightingales have decreased to
a very few birds during the last three or four
seasons ; and last summer (1897) the wood-wren
failed to put in an appearance. To say that
there will be other and greater changes is
unhappily only too safe a prophecy to make.
For several years past tree-felling has been
vigorously prosecuted in the gardens to give
them a more open park-like appearance ; new
gravelled roads have been laid down in all
directions, and the policy generally has been
that of the landscape-gardener which makes for
prettiness, with the result that the aspect and
character of this spot have been quite altered,
and it is fast becoming as unsuitable a breeding
place for the summer warblers and other shy
woodland species as any royal west-end park.

Up till two months ago, it was some consolation to those who grieved at the changes in
progress in Kew Gardens to think that the
Queen's private grounds adjoining were safe
from the despoiler. This area is separated
from the gardens by nothing but a wire fence ;
one could walk the entire breadth of the grounds
with that untrimmed, exquisitely beautiful

wooded wilderness always in sight ; many acres
of noble trees—oak, ash, elm, beech, hornbeam,
and Spanish chestnut ; a shady paradise, the
old trunks draped with ivy, or grey and emerald
green with moss ; masses of bramble and brier,
furze and holly, growing untouched beneath ;
the open green spaces a sea of blue in spring
with the enchanting blue of the wild hyacinth.
There was not anywhere on the borders of
London—that weary circuit of fifty miles—so
fresh and perfect a transcript of wild woodland
nature as this, with the sole exception of Lord
Mansfield's private grounds at Hampstead.

Unhappily just before the announcement
was made early in 1898 that the Queen had
graciously decided to admit the public to this
lovely ground, a gang of labourers was sent in
to grub up the undergrowth, to lop off lower
branches. and cut down many scores of the
noblest old trees, with the object apparently of
bringing the place more into harmony with the
adjoining trim gardens. It is earnestly to be
hoped that nothing further will be done to ruin
the most perfect beauty-spot that remains to
London.

Here our survey ends.

CHAPTER XIV

PROTECTION OF BIRDS IN THE PARKS

Object of this book—Summary of facts contained in previous
chapters—An incidental result of changes in progress—Some
degree of protection in all the open spaces, efficient protection in none—Mischievous visitors to the parks—Bird
fanciers and stealers—The destructive rough—The barbarians are few—Two incidents at Clissold Park—Love of
birds a common feeling of the people.

THE most serious portion of my work still remains to do. In the introductory chapter I
said that this was a book with a purpose, and,
as the reader knows from much that has gone
before, the purpose is to point out how the wild
bird life we possess may be preserved, and how
it may be improved by the addition of other
suitable species which would greatly increase
the attractiveness of the parks.

Before going into this part of my subject it
would be useful to briefly summarise the main
facts disclosed in the foregoing chapters.

1. Many species formerly resident through-

out the year in London have quite died out ;
thus, in the present century the following large

CHAFFINCH

species have been lost : raven, magpie, peregrine
falcon, and kestrel. In very recent years the
following small resident species have disappeared
from inner London, but are still found in a few

localities on the outskirts : missel-thrush, nut-hatch, tree-creeper, oxeye, and lesser spotted woodpecker.

2. Some resident species are reduced to small remnants and are confined to one or to a very few spots; in this category we must place the rook, the jackdaw, and the owl.

3. Several other resident species, formerly common, have greatly decreased in numbers, and in some of the open spaces appear to be dying out. Among these are the thrush, black-bird, robin, wren, hedge-sparrow, greenfinch, chaffinch, goldfinch, bullfinch, linnet, and lark. Two of these species, thrush and blackbird, are now increasing in several of the open spaces under the County Council, and here and there two or three of the other species named are also increasing.

4. The decrease has been in most, but not all, of the old residents. So far the carrion crow does not appear to have suffered. Two small birds, sparrow and starling, have un-doubtedly greatly increased.

5. At the same time that some of the old residents have been decreasing or dying out, a few other species have come in from the outside,

and have greatly increased—namely, the ring-dove, moorhen, and dabchick.

6. During the season when birds migrate, or shift their quarters, many birds of various species drift into or pass through London : of these some that are summer visitors bred regularly in London up to within a few years ago. Of all these visitors it may be said that they have been decreasing for several years past, and some of them no longer attempt to breed in the inner London parks. At the same time, in a few favoured localities these visitors do not show any falling off, and in one or two of the open spaces they may be actually increasing.

To sum up. For many years there have been constant changes going on in the bird population, many species decreasing, a very few remaining stationary, and a few new colonists appearing ; but, generally speaking, the losses greatly exceed the gains.

One incidental result of all these changes, and of the variety of conditions existing and the different degrees of protection given, is that some of the open spaces are now distinguished by the possession of species which are found

in no other spot in the metropolis, or which
have elsewhere become exceedingly rare. Thus,
Kensington Gardens alone, of all the interior
parks, possesses the owl and the jackdaw ; St.
James's Park is distinguished by its large number of wood-pigeons and its winter colonies
of black-headed gulls ; Battersea Park by its
wrens and variety of small delicate songsters,
both resident and migratory, and its vast con-
gregation of starlings in late summer and early
autumn ; Wandsworth Common by its yellow-
hammers ; Gray's Inn Gardens and Brockwell
Park by their rookeries ; Streatham by its
nightingales, magpies, and jays ; Ravenscourt
Park by its missel-thrushes ; Finsbury Park by
its large numbers of thrushes and blackbirds.
In Kew Gardens the tree-pipit, pied wagtail,
and wryneck are more common than elsewhere ;
Richmond Park has its heronry and a vast
multitude of daws ; Wanstead has the turtle-
dove and hawfinch, and with its land and water
birds of all sizes, from the goldcrest to the
heron, mallard, and rook, may claim to possess
in its narrow limits a more abundant and varied
wild bird life than any other metropolitan open
space.

The conclusion I have come to, after a careful study of the subject, is that wild birds of all the species remaining to us, and many besides, are very well able to thrive in London; that many species have been and are being lost solely on account of the indifference of the park authorities in the matter; that the comparative abundance and variety of wild bird life in the different open spaces depends on the degree of protection and encouragement the birds receive. And by encouragement I mean the providing them with islands, shrubberies, and such cover as they require when breeding. Thus, we see that in so vast a space as Hyde Park, where there is practically no protection given and nothing done to encourage wild birds, the songsters are few and are decreasing; while in some comparatively small open spaces constantly thronged with visitors the bird life is abundant and varied, and increasing. It should not be, but certainly is, the case that it depends on the person who is in charge of the open space whether anything shall be done to encourage the birds; if he takes no interest in the matter those who are under him will not concern themselves to save the birds. We have seen that veiled

bird-catching is permitted in some of the parks ;
park constables and park labourers have also
been allowed to take nests of thrushes and other
songsters containing young birds, for their own
pleasure or to dispose of to others.

We have seen that the differences between
park and park, with regard to the abundance of
bird life, are very great ; but despite these differences, which depend on the amount of encouragement and protection given, consequently
to a great extent on the personal feeling in the
matter of the superintendent, it must be said that
sufficient protection has not yet been given in any
public space in London. All the open spaces are
alike infested by cats, the deadliest enemy of
the birds which are of most value—the resident
species that sing most of the year, and that nest
in low bushes or close to the ground. And so
long as cats are allowed to range about the
parks these species cannot be said to be
properly protected. This last point being of
great importance will be treated separately and
fully in the next chapter ; the rest of this
chapter will be occupied in discussing an enemy
to the birds less difficult to deal with—the
mischievous individuals of our own species

WIMBLEDON COMMON

NEST OF CHAFFINCH

who kill and capture birds and take their eggs and young.

The damage done by the ordinary boy, who throws stones and cannot resist the temptation to take a nest when he has the chance, is hardly appreciable in the parks where there is any real desire on the part of the superintendents and keepers to protect the birds. On some of the large open spaces on the outskirts of London, such as Hampstead Heath and the commons in the South-west district, the keepers are too few to protect the nesting birds, and the eggs are very nearly all taken. A much more serious injury is inflicted by the bird fancier from the slums, who visits the parks with the object of stealing the birds, adults and young, and by the worst kind of blackguard or rough, who kills and smashes when he gets the chance solely for the pleasure of destroying something which others value, or, to quote Bacon's phrase, ' because he can do no other.'

As to the bird fancier who is a bird stealer, I have said enough in a former chapter to show that he can very easily be got rid of where there is any real desire to protect the birds.

It remains to say something concerning the

rough who delights in destruction. That a man
should find pleasure in stoning a valuable park
bird to death or in trampling down a flower-bed
may seem an astonishing thing, when we see
that the objects destroyed are solely intended for
the people's pleasure, that they are paid for by the
people, and are, in a sense, the people's property.
It may even seem inexplicable, since the rough
is a human being and must therefore have the
social instinct. But there is really no mystery
in it; by inflicting injury on the community he
is after all only following other instincts common
to man, which are quite as strong and sometimes
stronger than the social. He is prompted by
the hunting instinct, which is universal and
doubtless in him is to some extent perverted;
also the love of adventure, since by doing wrong
he runs a certain risk, and wins a little glory of
a low kind from his associates and others who are
of like mind with him; and finally, he is actuated
by the love of power, which in its degraded
form finds a measure of gratification in hurting
others, or in depriving them of a pleasure.

But after all said, these injurious persons are
in an exceedingly small, an almost infinitesimal,
minority, and the damage they do is little and

annually becomes less ; so little is it where any
vigilance is exercised, that it would not have
been worth while to write even these few para-
graphs but for the opportunity it gives me of
returning to a subject dwelt upon in the opening
chapter ; ·for this destructiveness on the part of
a few but serves the more fully to illustrate the
contrary spirit—-the keen and kindly interest in
the wild bird life of our open spaces which is
almost universal among the people. In the
volume dealing with East London, in his enormous work on the 'Life and Labour of the
People,' Mr. Charles Booth has the following
significant passage : ' The hordes of barbarians
of whom we have heard, who, issuing from their
slums, will one day overwhelm modern civilisa-
tion, do not exist. There are barbarians, but
they are a handful, a small and decreasing
percentage, a disgrace but not a danger.' A
more absolute confirmation of the truth of these
words than the general behaviour of the people
who visit the parks, even in the poorest and
most congested districts, could not be found.
As a rule, when a small park is first opened in
some densely populated district, where no public
open space previously existed, the people rush

in and act as if demented; they are like children
released from long confinement who go wild with
the first taste of liberty : they shout, climb trees,
break off branches, pluck the flowers; but all
this is purely the result of a kind of mental
intoxication.   They are not ' barbarians ' or
' yahoos,' as they are sometimes described by
onlookers at the first opening of a new park ;
they are nothing more than excited young
people ; the excitement passes, and after a short
time the damage ceases, and the place becomes
so orderly, and so seldom is any damage done,
that the park could almost be left to take care
of itself.

I am here tempted to relate two incidents
which have occurred at different times in one
small open space—Clissold Park. Some tame
rooks were kept with the object of establishing
a rookery (of which more in a later chapter), and
one day last year some young miscreants, who
subsequently made their escape, stoned three of
the birds to death.   The second incident relates
to a chaffinch and its nest.   The nest was
built on a stunted half-dead thorn-bush, very low
down and much exposed to sight.   Just at the
time when the nest was being built some forty

or fifty labourers were called in and set to work
to form a pond at this very spot, and it was
determined to leave a few yards of ground with
the thorn-bush standing on it as an island in the
middle of the excavation. When the digging
began the first eggs had been laid in the nest, but
in spite of the crowd of men at work every day and
all day long round the bush, and the incessant
noises of loud talking and of shovelling clay into
carts and shouting of carters to their horses, the
birds did not forsake their task ; the eggs were all
laid, sat on, the young duly hatched and successfully reared amidst the tumult ; and during all
this time the men engaged on the work were so
jealous of the birds' safety that they would not
allow any of the numberless visitors to the park
to come near the bush to look closely at the
nest. So long as the young were in the nest
the workmen were the chaffinch's bodyguard.

Judging from personal knowledge of the
people of London, I should say that these workmen showed in their action the feeling which the
people have generally about the wild birds in the
parks, and that the rook-slayers mentioned
above were rare exceptions, the small percentage
of ruffians which we always have to count with,

just as we have to count with lunatics and
criminals.   Doubtless some readers will disagree
with this conclusion.   I know it is a common
idea—one hears it often enough-—that love of
birds is by no means a general feeling ; that it is,
on the contrary, somewhat rare, and consequently
that those who experience it have some reason
to be proud of their superiority.   To my mind
all this is a pretty delusion ; no one flatters
himself that he is in any special way a lover of
sunshine and green flowery meadows and running waters and shady trees ; and I can only
repeat here what I have said before, that the
delight in a wild bird is as common to all men
as the feeling that the sunshine is sweet and
pleasant to behold.

One word more may be added here.   We—
that is to say, our representatives on the County
Council—annually spend some thousands of
pounds on gardening, in laying out beds of
brilliant tulips, geraniums, and other gay flowers,
but, with the exception of the cost of the little
food given to the birds in frosty weather in some
of the parks, not one pound, not one penny,
has been spent directly on the birds ; and yet
there is no doubt that the birds are more to most

people than the flowers ; that a gorgeous bed of tulips that has cost a lot of money is regarded by a majority of visitors with a very tepid feeling of admiration compared with that which they experience at the sight or sound, whether musical or not, of any wild bird.

CHAPTER XV

THE CAT QUESTION

As it will be necessary to show that, sooner or
later, the cat question will have to be dealt with
in a manner not pleasant for the cats, it may be
well to say at once that I have no prejudice
against this creature ; on the contrary, of all the
lower animals that live with or near us I admire
him the most, because of his incorruptibility, his
strict adherence to the principle ' to thine own
self be true.'   He lives with but not exactly in
subjection to us.   The coarser but more plastic
dog we can and we do in a sense unmake and
remake.   Not so with the cat, who keeps to the

terms of his ancient charter, in spite of all temptations to allow of a few of the original lines being rubbed out and some new ones written in their place. Old Æsop's celebrated apologue is as true of to-day as of his own distant time ; and thousands of years ago the worshippers of Pasht who had tender hearts must have been scandalised at their deity's way with a mouse. It would not, perhaps, be quite in order to conclude this exordium without a reference to the poet's familiar description of the cat as a ' harmless necessary ' animal. The Elizabethan was doubtless only thinking of rats and mice ; in the London of to-day the cat has another important use in keeping down the sparrows. But for this check sparrows would quickly become an intolerable nuisance, fluttering in crowds against our window-panes, crying incessantly for crumbs, and distressing us with the spectacle of their semi-starved condition.

Much has already been said of the sparrow in this work, but the lives of cat and sparrow are so interlaced in London that in speaking of one it becomes necessary to say something of the other. Let us try to get a little nearer to the subject of the connection between these

two creatures. When we consider the extreme
abundance of the sparrow in all favourable
situations and his general diffusion over the entire
metropolis ; that he inhabits thousands of miles
of streets, often many scores of birds to the
mile ; and that besides all the birds that breed
in houses others nest in trees and bushes in
every garden, square, park, and other open
space, we cannot suppose that there are less
than a million of these birds.   One day in April,
while walking rapidly the length of one walk in
a London park I counted 118 nests.   There
could not have been fewer than 1,000 nests
in the whole park.   The entire sparrow population of London may be as much as two or
three millions, or even more.   Putting it as low as
one million, the increase of half a million pairs,
breeding say four times a year, and rearing at
least twelve young (they often rear double that
number), we have an annual increase of six
millions.   Most of this increase goes to the cats ;
for the cat is the sparrow's sole enemy, but a
really dangerous one only when the bird is just out
of the nest ; for the young bird very soon becomes
strong of wing and alert in mind, and is thereafter
comparatively safe from the slayer of his kind.

The first instinct of the young urban sparrow, once he has been coaxed by his parents or impelled by something in him to use his wings, is to fly feebly, or rather to flutter downwards to the earth ; and there, under a bush in a back garden, or behind a pillar, or in an angle of the wall, or in the area, the cat is waiting. The inexperienced birdling, surprised and probably frightened at a new and strange sensation, trying to balance himself and to come down softly, touches the ground and is struck by sudden death. I have seen successive broods from one nest come forth, and bird by bird at odd times flutter down in this way, seeking a safer spot to rest upon than the sloping roof and narrow ledges and cornices on the walls, and finally touch the earth only to be instantly destroyed. But here one interesting question arises. How, if the facts are as stated, it may be asked, does it happen that the young sparrow so frequently makes this fatal mistake, in spite of his inherited knowledge ? I believe the explanation is that the sparrow is essentially a tree bird, notwithstanding his acquired habit of sitting contentedly on buildings in towns. A percher by nature, he is yet able to rub along

for most of the time without a perch ; but we
see that even in districts where trees are few
and far between the sparrows' meeting-place
or ' chapel ' is invariably a tree. The young
sparrow has not yet acquired this convenient
habit of the adults ; he is a tree sparrow,
incapable of sitting quietly, like the young
swallow or martin, on a roof or ledge to be fed
there by the parent birds. His perching feet
must lay hold of something ; and when he cannot, so to speak, anchor himself he is ill at ease,
even on the wide surface of a flat roof, and
fidgets and hops this way and that, possibly
experiencing a sensation as of falling or of
being thrown off his stand. It is to escape
from this unsuitable flat surface that he flutters
or flies off and comes down. This happens
when no tree stands conveniently near ; when
there is a tree beneath or close by the young
sparrow makes for it instinctively, as a duckling
to water ; and if he succeeds in reaching it he
shows at once that he has found relief, and is
content to remain where he is. It is most
interesting to watch a brood of young sparrows
just out of the nest settling down on the top-
most twigs of a tree, which they have been

lucky enough to reach, and remaining there for hours at a stretch, dozing secure in the sun and wind, even when the wind is strong enough to rock the tree, and only opening their eyes and rousing themselves at intervals on the appearance of one of the parent birds with food in its bill.

In a large majority of cases the London sparrow has no tree growing conveniently near to the breeding hole, and the consequence is that an incredible number of broods are lost. The parent birds, when a whole brood has thus been snapped up, after a day or two of excitement cheerfully set to work relining the old nest with a few straws, feathers, and hairs. From March to August, some to October, they are occupied with this business, and I do not think that more than two young birds survive out of every dozen of all the sparrows that breed in houses ; for. with the park birds the case is different. As it is, the birds that escape their subtle enemy are more than enough to make good the annual losses from all other causes. In the streets, back-yards, and gardens an ailing sparrow is, like the inexperienced young bird, quickly snapped up. In the parks at all seasons, but particularly in winter, ailing sparrows are not very rare; occasionally a dead one is seen.

> The duck and the drake
> Are there at his wake,

but the cat comes not in the daylight hours to bury him. When the young park sparrows flutter down from their high nests there is no enemy lying in wait : they get their proper exercise, and in short flights over the turf learn the use of their wings ; in the evening they go back to their hollow tree or inaccessible nest. When they are asleep in their safe cradles the cats come on the scene to hunt in the shrubberies, to capture the thrush, blackbird, robin, dunnock, and wren, and in fact any bird that nests in low bushes or on the ground. The noisy clang of the closing park gates is a sound well known to the cats in the neighbourhood ; no sooner is it heard than they begin to issue from areas and other places where they have been waiting, and in some spots as many as half a dozen to a dozen may be counted in as many minutes crossing the road and entering the park at one spot. They can go in anywhere, but cats that are neighbours and personally known to one another often have the habit of going in at one place. All night long they are at their merry games; you may sometimes see them scampering over the turf playing with one another like wild rabbits, and in the breeding season they sup on many an incubating bird caught on its eggs, and on many a nest full of fledglings. In the early morning they are back at their houses, if they are not of the homeless ones, innocently washing their faces in the breakfast room, waiting for the customary caress and saucer of cream. But these luxuries do not alter the animal's nature: his 'fearful symmetry' was for all time, the sinews of his heart cannot be twisted in any other way, and his brain is as it came from the furnace.

The following incident will serve to show the spirit that is in a London cat. Some time ago it was discovered that a very big and a very black one had established himself on an island in the lake at Battersea Park. 'Then he must have crossed over in a boat, as cats don't swim,' cried the superintendent. On going to the place it was found that the cat had killed and partly devoured one tufted duck and two

sheldrakes.   To dispose of him a company of
eighteen workmen and a good hunting dog were
sent over to the island.   The cat, driven from his
hiding-place in the bushes, quickly ascended the
tallest tree in his territory.   A youth who was
a good climber went up after him, and the other
men, armed with stout sticks, gathered round the
tree to receive the animal on his coming down.
The cat quickly made up his mind how to act :
down he swiftly came from branch to branch,
and in less than two seconds was frantically
tearing about among the legs of his adversaries,
and bursting through the cordon was quickly in
the water swimming for life.   Immediately there
was a rush for the boats, but before the men
could get on to the water the cat had reached
the shore and vanished in the thick shrubbery.
The men were then disposed in line like beaters
and advanced, but in the end the creature escaped
from the park and was lost.   This animal deserves
honourable mention on account of the splendid
courage and resource he displayed ; but the
injury he had caused and the desperate and
successful fight for life he made against such
tremendous odds show that cats ought not to be
allowed in the parks.   The loss of the pair of

PARK SPARROWS

MOORHEN AND CHICKS

sheldrakes is felt to be a serious one, and I agree that when unpinioned the bird is very beautiful, and when it shows itself flying over the ornamental waters of a park, I can admire it almost as much as when seeing it on the coasts of Somerset or Northumberland. But a blackcap, a nightingale, a kingfisher destroyed by cats in any park would be as great or even a greater loss to London; and I may add that a few days before writing this chapter, in the summer of 1897, the three wild birds I have just named were to be seen at the very spot where the sheldrakes were killed.

So far as I know, the park cats can only be credited with one good deed. Two or three years ago a number of rabbits were introduced into Hyde Park, and quickly began to increase and multiply, as rabbits will. For a time the cats respected them, being unaccustomed to see such animals, and possibly thinking that they would be dangerous to tackle. But they soon found out that these strangers were the natural prey of a carnivore, and, beginning with the little ones, then going on to those that were grown up, eventually devoured them all. Two big old buck rabbits survived the others for a couple of months, but even these were finally conquered and eaten. I for one am very glad at the result, for it really seemed too ridiculous that our great national park should be turned into a rabbit warren as well as a duck-breeding establishment.

The extraordinary rapidity with which the rabbits were destroyed will serve to give some idea of the numbers and destructiveness of the cats that nightly make the open spaces of London their hunting grounds. How many cats are there in London? Not a word that I am aware of has been written on the subject, and as there is no tax on them there is no possibility of finding out the exact truth. Nevertheless, in an indirect way we may be able to get a proximate idea of their numbers.

The number of dogs in London is supposed to be about two hundred thousand; no doubt it is really greater, since many dogs escape the tax. Cats in London are very much more numerous than dogs. Thus, in the streets I know best, in the part of London where I live, there are about eight cats to every dog; in some streets there are ten or twelve, in others not more than six. If a census could be taken it would probably show that the entire cat population does not fall short of three-quarters of a million ; but I may be wide of the mark in this estimate, and should prefer at present to say that there are certainly not less than half a million cats in London. Even this may seem an astonishing number, since it is not usual for any house to have more than one, and in a good many houses not one is kept. On the other hand there is a vast population of ownerless cats. These cannot well be called homeless since they all attach themselves to some house, which they make their home, and to which they return as regularly as any wild beast to its den or lair. Judging solely from my own observation, I do not think that there can be less than from eighty thousand to one hundred thousand of these ownerless cats in the metropolis. Let me take the case of the house I live in. No cat is kept, yet from year's end to year's end there are seldom less than three cats to make use of it, or to make it their home. At all hours of the day they are to be seen in the area, or on the doorsteps, or somewhere near ; and at odd times they go into the basement rooms— they get in at the windows, or at any door that happens to be left open, and if not discovered spend the night in the house. There are scores of houses in my immediate neighbourhood which have no smell of valerian about them and are favoured in the same way.

It is not possible at all times of the year to distinguish these ownerless or stray cats from those that have owners; but there are seasons of scarcity for the outdoor animals during which they differ in appearance from the others; and at such times, with some practice, one may get an idea of the number of strays in his own neighbourhood. It is in the winter, during long and severe frosts, that the ownerless ones suffer most, and on a bright day in a walk of a quarter of a mile you will sometimes see as many as a dozen of these poor wretches sunning themselves on one side of the street. On coming close to one of these cats he invariably looks at you with wide-open startled eyes, and so long as you stand quietly regarding him he will keep this look. The moment you speak kindly to him the alarm vanishes from his eyes, he knows you for a friend, and is as ready as any starving human beggar to tell you his miserable story. He mews piteously; but sometimes when his mouth opens no sound issues from it—he is too feeble even to mew. His fur has a harsher appearance than in other cats, the hairs stand up like the puffed-out feathers of an owl, and hide his body's excessive leanness; but when you lift him up you are astonished at his lightness—he is like a wisp of straw in your hand. The marvel is that when he has got to this pass he can still keep alive from day to day; for in the bleak streets there is no food for him, and the people of the houses he hangs about have hardened their hearts against him on account of his thieving, or because if they give him an occasional scrap of food he will never go away, and their only wish is to see the last of him. Many of these stray cats get most of their food in dust-bins, into which they slink whenever the door is left open for a few minutes. They find a few scraps to keep them alive, and at rare intervals capture a mouse. Sometimes they jump out when ashes are shot into their hiding-place; but the cat who has got hardened merely shuts his eyes against the stinging cloud, crouching in his corner, and is satisfied to remain for days shut up in his dreary cell, finding it more tolerable than the

wintry streets and inhospitable areas.   It is
related of La Fontaine, the fabulist, that he was
passionately fond of strawberries, on account
of the effect which this fruit had in annually
restoring him to comparative health and some
pleasure in life ; and that during the winter and
spring his only wish was that the strawberry
season when it came round again would find
him still living, since if it delayed its coming
he would lose all hope.   In like manner these
ownerless cats, if they have any thought about
their condition, must long for the change in the
year that will once more call forth the black-
beetles in areas and basements, and bring the
young sparrows fluttering down from their
inaccessible nests.

How does it happen that there are so many
of these strays in London ?   For cats do not leave
their homes of their own accord, except in rare
instances when they have been enticed or encouraged to take up their quarters in some other
neighbourhood.   As a rule the animal prefers
its own home with poverty to abundance in a
strange place.   I believe that a vast majority
of these poor ones come from the houses or
rooms inhabited by the poor.   Most persons are

extremely reluctant to put kittens that are not wanted to death. In the houses of the well-to-do the servants are ordered to kill them; but the poor have no person to delegate the dirty work to ; and they have, moreover, a kindlier feeling for their pet animals, owing to the fact that they live more with them in their confined homes than is the case with the prosperous. The consequence is that in very many cases not one of a litter is killed ; they are mostly given away to friends, and their friends' children are delighted to have them as pets. The kitten amuses a child immensely with its playful ways, and is loved for its pretty blue eyes full of fun and mischief and wonder at everything. But when it grows up the charm vanishes, and it is found that the cat is in the way ; he is often on the common staircase where there are perhaps other cats, and eventually he becomes a nuisance. The poor are also often moving, and are not well able to take their pet from place to place. It is decided to get rid of the cat, but they do not kill it, nor would they like to see it killed by another ; it must be ' strayed '—that is to say, placed in a sack, taken for some miles away from home at night and released in a strange place.

Now this very painful condition of things ought not to continue, and my only reason for going into the subject is to suggest a remedy. This is that the metropolitan police be instructed to remove all stray cats and send them to a lethal chamber provided for the purpose. The ownerless cats, we have seen, do not roam about the town, but have a home, or at all events a house, to which they attach themselves, and which they refuse to leave, however inhospitably or even cruelly they may be treated. On making some inquiries at houses in my own neighbourhood on the subject, I find that most people are anxious to get rid of the stray cats they may happen to have about the place, but are at a loss to know how to do it. In some instances they succeed in straying them again, but the cats are no better off than before, and the starving population is not diminished. But it would be a simple way out of the difficulty if they could have them removed by reporting them to the nearest policeman. We have seen, as a result of the muzzling order imposed by the County Council, that upwards of forty thousand unclaimed dogs have been destroyed in the course of a year (1896), and the presumption is that these dogs were little valued and not properly cared for by their owners. The harvest of stray cats would probably not be less than sixty or seventy thousand for the first year.

To return to the parks. The question is how to exclude the hunting cats that frequent them at night. I have conversed with perhaps a hundred superintendents, inspectors, and keepers on the subject, and invariably they say that it is impossible to exclude the cats, or that they do not see how it is to be done. And yet in many parks they are always trying to do it; they hunt them at night with dogs, they shoot them with rook rifles, and they poison them; but all these measures produce no effect, and are, moreover, employed with secrecy and with fear lest the paragraph writer and public should find out, and an outcry be made. It is plain that the cats can only be kept out by means of a suitable fence, or net, or screen of wire. Rabbit wire netting is hardly suitable, as it is unsightly and is not an efficient protection. The most effectual form would be a plain wire fence in squares, the cross wires tied to the uprights with wire thread, the top of the fence made to curve outwards to prevent the animals from climbing over it. This screen could be placed inside of the park railings at a distance of about three or four feet from them. A fence or screen of this pattern has a handsome appearance, but it is expensive, the cost being about fourpence to fivepence the square foot. Probably some other cheaper and equally effective wire protection could be designed. I have consulted some of the large dealers in wire netting and fencing of all kinds, and they tell me that a fence to keep out cats from parks has yet to be invented. Very likely; at the same time there are probably very many ingenious persons in England who would quickly invent what is wanted if it was made worth their while. It simply comes to this: if the park authorities really wish to keep out the cats they can do so at a moderate cost, and it is not likely that even their worst critics would venture to blame them for spending a few hundreds for such an object.

We must look to the County Council to take the lead in this matter. It is my conviction— there is much even now going on in some of the parks to show how well founded it is—that once the chief destroyer of our valuable birds is excluded, a great and rapid improvement in the character of our bird population will ensue. The number of the species we value most would be relatively larger. The change for the better would come about without any direct encouragement and protection being given ; at the same time it would be an immense help if those who are in charge of open spaces could be brought to see that wild bird life is very much more to the people of London than all the pleasant and pretty things in the way of bands of music, exotic flowers, and brick and stone and metal ornaments, which they are providing at a very considerable cost.

STARLING

CHAPTER XVI

BIRDS FOR LONDON

Restoration of the rook—The Gray's Inn rookery—Suggestions
—On attracting rooks—Temple Gardens rookery—Attempt
to establish a rookery at Clissold Park—A new colony of
daws—Hawks—Domestic pigeons—An abuse—Stock-dove
and turtle-dove—Ornamental water-fowl, pinioned and
unpinioned—Suggestions—Wild water-fowl in the parks—
Small birds for London—Missel-thrush—Nuthatch—Wren
—Loudness a merit—Summer visitants to London—Kingfisher—Hard-billed birds—A use for the park sparrows—
Natural checks—A sanctuary described.

My purpose in this chapter is to make a few
suggestions as to the species which may be
introduced or restored with a fair prospect of
success, and which would form a valuable addition to the metropolitan wild bird life. The
species to be mentioned here have very nearly
all been resident, some of them very common, in
former years ; most of them survive on the
borders of London, and some still linger in
diminished numbers in a few of the interior open
spaces.

Most persons would probably agree that of all the large birds that were once common in London, the rook would be most welcome. In the chapter on this bird I said that irretrievable disaster had overtaken the London rookeries, that the birds had gone, or were going, never to return ; nevertheless, I believe that it would be possible, although certainly not easy, to reintroduce them. We have not wholly lost the rook yet ; he is to be found in many places on our borders ; and the continued existence of the ancient colony at Gray's Inn is a proof that rooks can live in London, and would doubtless be able to thrive in some of the parks where there are large trees, and from which the birds would not have to travel so far in search of food for their young. With regard to the Gray's Inn rooks, which are greatly valued by the Benchers and by very many others, I will venture to make a suggestion or two, which, if acted on, may produce good results. Probably no bird from outside is ever attracted to this colony, confined to so small an open space in the very heart of London, and it is possible that through too much in-and-in breeding for many generations, the birds have suffered a considerable loss of vigour. It would be a very easy matter to infuse fresh blood into it by substituting eggs from some country rookery for those in the nests. This experiment would cost nothing ; and it would also be worth while to provide the birds with suitable provender, such as meal-worms, at the season when the young are growing and require more food than the parents are probably able to give them.

No doubt some readers of this book will say at once that the reintroduction of the rook into London is impossible, since even in the rural districts, where all the conditions are favourable, it is found extremely difficult to induce the birds to settle where they are wanted. A year or two ago my friend Mr. Cunninghame Graham, writing from his place in the north, told me that he had long desired to have rooks in his trees, and that he had written to an eminent ornitho-logist, with whom he was not personally ac-quainted, asking for advice in the matter. The naturalist replied at some length, pointing out the fallacies of Socialism as a political creed, but saying nothing about the rooks. Probably he had nothing practical to write on the subject, but he might at least have informed his corre-

spondent that Mr. Hawker, the famous parson
of Morwenstow, had got his rooks by praying for
them. He prayed every day for three years,
and his importunity was then rewarded by
the birds coming and settling on the very trees
where they were wanted.

We have an account of the curious origin
of the Temple Gardens rookery, one of the best
known and most populous of the old London
rookeries. In the ' Zoologist,' vol. xxxvi. p. 196,
Mr. Harting relates that it was founded in
Queen Anne's time by Sir Richard Northey, a
famous lawyer at that period, who brought the
first birds from his estate at Epsom. A bough
was cut from a tree with a nest containing two
young birds, and conveyed in an open waggon
to the Temple, and fixed in a tree in the gardens.
The old birds followed their young and fed them,
and old and young remained and bred in the
same place. The following year a magpie built
in the gardens ; her eggs were taken, and those
of a rook substituted ; these in due course
were hatched and the young when reared became
an addition to the colony.

Professor Newton has said of this pleasant
story that he would gladly believe it if he could,

and it has been discredited by the discovery
that a rookery existed at the Temple prior to
Queen Anne's time. Aubrey's statement, which
has been quoted in disproof of the Northey
legend, is that the rooks built their nests there
in the spring after the plague, 1665. My
inference is that the rookery was an old one,
which the birds abandoned during the plague,
and afterwards reoccupied. We may then
suppose that later on the birds went away again
for good ; and that Northey, knowing that a
rookery had formerly existed at the Temple,
and inspired by a lawyer's very natural admiration for the grave, black-coated, contentious
bird, succeeded in restoring it in the manner
described. In any case, it is not probable that
such a story would have been told of the
Temple rookery if the plan attributed to Northey
had not been successfully employed somewhere
and somewhen. It is well worth trying again.
I should like very much to see the experiment
made by Lord Ilchester, who has long desired to
see the rooks back in Holland Park ; he would
not have to bring the young birds in their nests
in open waggons all the way from Melbury or
Abbotsbury, as there are several rookeries where

young birds in the nests could be had within
five or six miles of Holland House.

Another more promising plan is to get the
young birds and rear them in the park where
they are wanted. This plan has already been
recently tried, not by any person of means, but
by a humble park sergeant at Clissold Park.
Sergeant Kimber is an interesting man, and
deserves to be highly thought of by all bird-
lovers in London ; he has during most of his
life been a gamekeeper, but knows a great deal
more about birds and loves them better than
most men who have that vocation. With the
permission of the County Council, he obtained
about a dozen young rooks from the country,
some from Yorkshire and others from Wales ;
the birds were placed in an enclosure with a
good-sized tree growing in it with branches
drooping to the ground, so that they were able
to ascend and descend at pleasure. Unfortunately their wing feathers were cut, which prevented them from learning to fly for about a
year ; even after two years the survivors are still
unable to fly as well as wild birds. Six birds
remained up to the spring of 1897 ; one
only of these appeared to be a male. This

bird paired and a nest was built, but after its completion the pair flew away together one morning to some open ground on the outskirts of North London where they were accustomed to feed, and never returned. Doubtless they had been shot by the sportsmen who still infest the waste lands and marshes on that side of the metropolis. Sergeant Kimber now thinks that it was a mistake to clip his rooks' wings, and hopes to succeed better next time.

This experiment with tame rooks has incidentally resulted in a gain to the bird life of North London. In the aviary at Clissold Park a tame female daw was kept; there she formed a very close friendship with a parrot, who had the original way of manifesting, or perhaps I should say dissembling, his love by pulling out her feathers. No doubt she was very much enamoured of the green bird with his foreign ways and commanding voice, as she was always at his side and never in the least resented his ungentle treatment. The poor bird's breast was at last quite denuded of its covering, and the whole plumage was in such a thin and ragged condition that it was thought best to separate the friends, even at the risk of breaking their

hearts; accordingly the daw was taken away
and placed with the tame rooks. The rooks
treated her very well, and in their society she
probably soon forgot her foreigner. And by-
and-by a wild daw was attracted to the tree
and joined the company : this was a male bird
in fine plumage, and Sergeant Kimber conceived
the idea that it would be a good stroke to catch
it and clip its wing-tips to prevent it from going
away. The wild daw was very cunning; by
day he would remain most of the time with the
rooks and his ragged friend, but at night he
invariably retired to roost in some tall trees in
another part of the park. In spite of his
cunning he was eventually caught and placed
on the rooks' tree with just the tips of his wings
clipped. From that time the two daws were
inseparable, and their romantic attachment
promised to end in a lasting and happy union ;
but after a few weeks a second wild daw, this
time a female, was attracted to the tree and
joined the little community. This was a fine
glossy bird, and no sooner had she come than
the male daw began to make up to her, coolly
throwing over his first love. By this time he
had recovered his power of flight, and after

pairing with the new-comer the two went away
to spend the honeymoon and look for a suitable
residence in the country. The ragged daw lived
on with the rooks for a few weeks longer, then
she too disappeared, being now able to fly. Three
or four weeks later, to everybody's astonishment,
they all came back together accompanied by
a fourth bird, a male, with which the ragged one
had paired. Somewhere roaming about outside of
London they had all met, and the ragged female
had probably persuaded them to forget past
unpleasantnesses and return to the park ; at all
events they all seemed very friendly and happy.
During the summer of 1897 both pairs bred,
one in the upper part of the tall spire of St.
Mary's Church, Stoke Newington, which stands
close to the main entrance to the park ; the other
in a building close by.

We see from this that wandering and apparently homeless daws often visit London, and
are quickly attracted by any tame unconfined
bird of their own species ; and that where daws
are wanted, an excellent plan is to use a tame
bird as a decoy.

It is exceedingly improbable that any of
the raptorial species which formerly inhabited

London—peregrine falcon, kestrel, and kite—
will ever return, but we could have these birds
by rearing them by hand from the nest, and
allowing them to be unconfined. If well and
regularly fed they would remain where they were
reared, or if they went away for a season they
would most probably return. It would be a
great pleasure to see them soaring above or
about our buildings, and they would also be
useful in keeping down the domestic pigeons,
which are now much too numerous and are fast
becoming a nuisance in some of the parks, where
they devour the food originally intended for the
wood-pigeons. The domestic pigeons have a
pretty appearance at St. Paul's Cathedral, Westminster Palace, and other large public buildings;
in the grassy parks they are out of place and do
not look well; furthermore, when we find most,
if not all, of these park-haunting birds come from
big private houses in the neighbourhood, where
they are bred for the table, it is surprising that
the park authorities should continue to feed
them at the public expense. Let us hope that
this abuse will soon be put an end to ; also that
it will be recognised by the authorities that it is
a mistake to keep dovecots in the public parks.

The stock-dove could easily be introduced
into London by placing its eggs, which can be
obtained at a trifling cost, under both the
domestic pigeon and wood-pigeon. It may be
that the wood-pigeon would also prove a suitable
foster-parent to the turtle-dove. This species is
a strict migrant, but if bred in the parks it would
no doubt come back annually from its journeys
abroad. In any case the experiment is well
worth trying.

Before going on to the small birds which
may be introduced or encouraged to settle,
something need be said about the ornamental
water-fowl of the parks, which might be made
more than they are to us, and put to a new use.
There is no doubt that just as one daw attracts
other daws so do these water-birds attract
any of their wild relations which may be
passing at night. Mallards, widgeon, and teal,
supposed to be wild birds, have been known to
appear in some of the parks to pair with the
park birds and remain to breed; in a few
instances some of these strangers have actually
been captured by the keepers and pinioned to
prevent them from leaving. This was a great

mistake ; for assuming that the birds really were wild, it is probable that after going away for the winter they would have returned, and might even have brought some of their wild fellows. I believe that our ornamental water-fowl ought never to be pinioned except in the cases of a few rare exotic species. When a bird is pinioned its chief beauty and greatest charm are lost ; it is then little more than a domestic bird, or a bird in a cage. Sheldrakes, both common and ruddy, are infinitely more beautiful when flying than when resting on the water ; and all wild ducks are seen at their best when, before alighting, they sweep along close to the surface, with wings motionless and depressed, showing the bright beauty-spot. There are, in fact, many unpinioned fowls on the park waters, and some of these birds not only fly about their own ponds, but they occasionally visit the waters of other parks, especially by night, and are well able to find their way back to their own ponds. In some cases they make prolonged visits to other parks. In one London park for the last three years a number of tufted ducks (from eight to a dozen) have made their appearance on the ornamental water each spring, and

have remained until the autumn, then disappeared ; it is not known where they spend the
winter.   In the same park a pair of pinioned
ruddy sheldrakes were kept.   In April 1897
they were joined by a third bird, a drake, in
very beautiful plumage.   After being two or
three days in their company, he attacked the
pinioned drake with great fury and drove
him off, and took possession of the duck.
The ornamental water of another park has
been visited at odd times by several Egyptian
geese, sometimes appearing regularly every
morning and departing in the evening, at other
times making long stays; and I have heard of
many other instances of the kind.

There are many and good reasons for
believing that water-fowl hatched and reared in
the parks would, if they went away for a period
in autumn and winter, return in spring to breed.
A fair trial might be made by giving the eggs
of wild birds—widgeon, teal, gadwell, shoveller,
and other suitable British species, to the park
ducks when breeding.   In this way a London
race of each or of a few of these species might
be established ; like our black-headed gulls,
moorhens, and dabchicks, they would be wild

birds, although not shy, and they would certainly be more beautiful and vigorous and give us more pleasure than their pinioned relations. Coots hatched and reared by the moorhens would give us another wild bird well suited to thrive in the park lakes ; and I will venture to add that we might even get the great crested grebe, by placing its eggs in the dabchicks' nests. The breeding habits of these two species are identical ; they differ very considerably in size, but there is not so great a disparity between little grebe and great grebe as there is between the cuckoo and its foster-parent.

Of small birds, or songsters, it will not be necessary to mention more than a few of the species which might be introduced with advantage, since little can be done so long as the bird-killing cats are free of the parks, and little will need to be done once the cats are excluded. Such species as the robin and hedge-sparrow require protection when breeding ; they are now dying out for want of it, and will undoubtedly increase again whenever the park authorities think proper to give it.

The quickest and most effective plan to add

to the number of our species is to procure the
eggs of suitable wild birds, to be hatched in the
nests of the park birds.   Thus, the missel-thrush
might easily be got back by placing its eggs in
the nests of blackbirds and thrushes.   The large
size and handsome plumage of the missel-thrush,
or storm-cock, his dashing motions and loud
winter song, would make him one of our most
attractive birds ; and that he is well able to
thrive in London we have already seen.

Another bird which no one is ever tired of
seeing and hearing, and would be a great acquisition, is the nuthatch ; this species, although
not uncommon on the wooded borders of London
and in some of the outlying parks, would no
doubt have to be introduced by man.   The
nuthatch is a difficult bird to manage, on account
of its violent temper and impatience of confinement ; but it is possible that the starling, which,
like the nuthatch, breeds in hollow trees, and
feeds its young on much the same kind of food,
might make a suitable foster-parent.   At all
events, the experiment is worth trying.   It
should be easy to procure its eggs, as the bird
is very common in many well-timbered parks
and open oak woods within a short distance of

London. There are, I imagine, few small birds
more fitted to give pleasure to Londoners than
the nuthatch, on account of his quaint figure
and pretty plumage, his sprightliness and amusing squirrel-like movements on a trunk or
branch of a tree. Though not strictly a songster,
his various clear penetrative call-notes are very
delightful to hear; and he is most loquacious in
late winter and early spring, when bird-voices
are few. Furthermore, of wild birds that may
be taught to come to us for food he is one of the
quickest to learn, and will follow his feeder, or
come at call, and deftly catch the nuts and
crusts and fragments of any kind that are thrown
to him.

Two other small birds with loud bright voices
—both London species, but now very nearly
vanished, as we have seen—are the oxeye and
wren. I think the best plan with regard to
these two—and the same plan might be tried
with the nuthatch in the event of the starling's
failure as a foster-parent—would be to catch the
young birds shortly after leaving the nest, and
release them as soon as possible in the parks.
All these three have the habit of roosting in
families, old and young together, in a hole or

other sheltered place ; and if taken at night and released the following day where they were wanted, they would probably soon adapt themselves to their new surroundings.

The wren, indeed, appears to have more adaptiveness than most birds, being universal in the British Islands, and able to survive the cold and scarcity of the long northern winters, even in the most bleak and barren situations. That he is well able to thrive in London we know, in spite of the fact that he has now all but vanished from most of our open spaces ; for we have seen that in one park, within two miles of Charing Cross, where he is more encouraged and better protected than elsewhere, he is actually increasing in number. He is a delightful little bird, a very general favourite, and is a winter singer with a bright, beautiful, lyrical song, wonderfully loud for so tiny a creature. I was never more impressed with the loudness of its song than on one Sunday afternoon in the spring of 1897 in Battersea Park. I was walking with the park superintendent round the lake, listening for some new summer voice, but for some time no bird sound reached us. Fifty or sixty boats full of noisy rowers were on the water, and the walks were thronged with loudly talking and laughing people, their numberless feet tramping on the gravel paths producing a sound like that of a steam roller. My companion exclaimed impatiently that it was impossible to hear a bird-note in so much noise. He had scarcely spoken before a wren, quite fifty yards away, somewhere on the island opposite to us, burst out singing, and his bright lyric rang forth loud and clear and perfect above all that noise of the holiday crowd.

It would be extremely difficult, perhaps impossible, to introduce by artificial means any of the summer visitants in the absence of soft-billed birds to play the part of foster-parents. The hedge-sparrow, the best bird for such a task, is too rare ; should he increase again, the case will be different. At the same time it may be said that the better protection which alone would cause the hedge-sparrow and robin to increase would also attract the migrants to breed in the parks. At present, the summer songsters that come regularly to breed in various spots on the borders of London are the following : whinchat, stonechat, redstart, nightingale, whitethroat, lesser-whitethroat, blackcap, garden warbler, chiffchaff, willow-wren, wood-wren, sedge-warbler, reed-warbler, pied wagtail, and tree-pipit. All these species, excepting the wood-wren, visit the open spaces of inner London on migration in spring. The chats, redstart, and tree-pipit are much rarer than the others; but of the fourteen species named, at least eight can be seen or heard by any person who cares to spend two or three days in the parks, to watch and listen to the birds, after the middle of April. This list is limited to the species which I have no doubt would breed in the parks if encouraged; the three species of swallows, the wheatear, yellow wagtail, and other summer visitants are also seen in April in London, but these are simply passing through.

The kingfisher, singly and in pairs, has been a rather frequent visitor to the parks during the last two years, and in some instances has made a long stay : there is no doubt that the abundance of minnows in the ornamental waters and the shelter of the wooded islands are a great attraction. No instance of its attempting to breed has yet occurred, but this may be due to the want of a suitable place to nest in. It is possible that the noise of the Saturday and Sunday boating people in the larger lakes, and the persecution of the sparrows, who hate him for his brilliant dress, may drive him away ; still, it would be a good plan to construct an artificial bank or rockery, with breeding holes, on one of the islands at a suitable place like Battersea.

The hard-billed birds would no doubt be the easiest to introduce, owing to the large number of sparrows that nest in the park trees, from which the eggs could be taken and those of other species substituted ; and if by acting as foster-parents to other finches the sparrows would only be breeding crows to pick their own eyes out, as the proverb says, so much the better. Chaffinches and greenfinches have been success-fully reared by sparrows ; and to these two other equally desirable species might be added : yellowhammer, corn-bunting, reed-bunting, bull-finch, goldfinch, and linnet. These are charm-ing birds and good songsters ; even the corn-bunting, although generally belittled by its biographers, is, compared with the sparrow, an accomplished musician. They are furthermore all exceedingly hardy, and probably as well able to thrive in London as the sparrow itself, although not so prolific and pushing as that sometimes troublesome bird. It is, indeed, on account of their hardiness that they, or those of them that have the best voices, are so much sought after; for they will live and be lively, and sing, for a period of ten or a dozen years, even in the miserable prison of a little cage in which they are kept by those who love them.

The excessive numbers of sparrows in the parks, where, as we have seen, there is no natural check on their increase, is a question difficult to deal with, and no remedy that is not somewhat unpleasant to think of has yet been tried or suggested. In some of the parks the nests are pulled down by the hundred; but where this plan is followed it is said to be of little avail, owing to the energy and persistence of the birds in making fresh nests. In other parks the birds are, or have been, netted at night in the bushes, where they roost in crowds. Poisoning the sparrows has also probably been tried; at all events, in one park I have found the sparrows looking sick and languishing, and many dead birds lying about, as if an epidemic had broken out among them; but as no signs of disease could be detected in the birds outside the park, it could not very well have been an epidemic.

Now since all these methods, which, like the

little spasmodic attempts to kill the cats in some
of the parks, are practised in secrecy and fear
lest the public should hear of them, have so far
proved ineffectual, would it not be best to take
a lesson from Nature, and restore some of the
natural checks which we have taken away?
Let us in the first place make use of the park
sparrows in establishing colonies of as many new
or greatly diminished species as possible; and
when we have done this, let us further introduce,
in moderate numbers, such species as prey on
small birds and their eggs and young—peregrine
falcon, kestrel, sparrow-hawk, owl, crow, daw,
magpie, and jay.

However successful we may be in adding to
the number of our songsters, the sparrow will
always be more numerous than all the other
species together, and on account of his abundance he will be more preyed upon; furthermore, his big, conspicuous, slovenly nests will
be more subject to attack than the nests of
other species. It has been shown that millions
of sparrows are yearly destroyed by cats in
London; yet so quickly are they snapped up
by their subtle enemy that we really see nothing
or very little indeed of the process. The young

birds flutter out of their nests and drop lightly down, only to vanish like snowflakes that fall on the water. Here we see that even in London, with but two species to act upon, Nature, left a little to herself, has succeeded in establishing something like that balance of forces and harmony which exists everywhere in her own dominion. Would it not be better to leave it to Nature in the parks, too, to do her own killing in her own swift and secret manner? In streets and houses cats are of the greatest service, doing for us, and unseen by us, that which we could not effectually do for ourselves: in the parks their presence is injurious; there we rather want Nature's feathered executioners, who are among her most beautiful and interesting creatures.

How effective and salutary her methods are, how beautiful in their results, may be seen in such places as have been made sanctuaries for all wild animals, innocent and rapacious. Even on the borders of London we have such places, and perhaps it would be hard anywhere in the rural districts to find a more perfect sanctuary in a small space than that of Caen Wood, at Hampstead. Although at the side of the swarming Heath, it is really wild, since for long

years it has been free from the landscape gardener
with his pretty little conventions, and the
gamekeeper and henwife with their persecutions
and playing at Providence among the creatures.
If it were possible for a man to climb to the top
of one of its noble old trees—a tall cedar, beech,
or elm, with a girth of sixteen to eighteen feet—he
would look down and out upon London: leagues
upon leagues of houses, stretching away to the
southern horizon, with tall chimneys, towers, and
spires innumerable appearing above the brood-
ing cloud of smoke.   But the wood itself seems
not to have been touched by its sulphurous
breath ; within its green shade all is fresh as
in any leafy retreat a hundred miles from town.
And here the wild creatures find a refuge.
Badgers—not one pair nor two, but a big colony
—have their huge subterraneous peaceful village
in the centre of the wood.   The lodge-keeper's
wife told me that one evening, seeing her dog,
as she imagined, trotting from her across the
lawn, she called to him and, angered at his disregard of her voice, ran after him for some distance among the trees, and only when she was
about to lay her hands on him discovered that
she was chasing a big badger.   The badgers have

for neighbours stoats and weasels, carrion crows,
jays, and owls.   Even in the daytime you will find
the wood-owl dozing in the deep twilight of a
holly-bush growing in the shade of a huge oak
or elm.   High up on the trees at least half a
dozen pairs of carrion crows have their nests;
and occasionally all the birds gather at one
spot and fill the entire wood with their tremendous excited cries.   A dozen of these birds,
when they let themselves go, will create a greater
uproar than a hundred cawing rooks.

Here, too, the rabbit keeps his place in spite
of so many enemies ; and to those named must
be added the domestic cat.   I myself have seen
puss returning to the house carrying a half-grown
young rabbit to her kittens.

The moorhen and wood-pigeon also flourish,
and in a still greater degree the missel-
thrush, throstle, and blackbird.   In this wood I
have counted forty-three breeding species ; and
not only is the variety great, but many of our
best songsters, residents and migrants, are so
numerous that at certain times in spring, when
birds are most vocal, you may hear at this spot
as fine a concert of sweet voices as in any wood
in England.

Sanctuaries like that of Caen Wood the Metropolitan parks can never be. Only in a few of the most favourably situated open spaces on the borders of London could we have anything approaching to the richness and harmony seen in this perfect transcript of wild nature. But it should be our aim to have all the parks, even to the most central, as nearly like sanctuaries as such small isolated urban spaces, inhabited by so limited a number of species, may be made.

DABCHICK'S FLOATING NEST : ST. JAMES'S PARK

BIBLIOGRAPHY

JENNINGS (JAMES) : *Ornithologia ; or, the Birds ;* a poem in two parts, with an introduction to their Natural History and copious notes. Second edition, 8vo. London, 1829.

TORRE (H. J.) : ' A List of Birds found in Middlesex.' *The Naturalist* (Neville Wood's), vol. iii. p. 420.   8vo.   London, 1838.

HIBBERD (SHIRLEY) : ' London Birds.'   *Intellectual Observer*, vol. vii. pp. 167–175.   8vo.   London, 1865.

POWER (F. D.) : ' A List of Birds noticed in London during 1863–4.' *Zoologist*, vol. xxiii. p. 9,727.   London, 1865.

HARTING (J. E.) : *The Birds of Middlesex.*   8vo.   London, 1866.

ADAMS (A. LEITH) : ' Birds of London.'   *Field*, January 16 and 23. London, 1875.

HAMILTON (EDWARD) : ' The Rooks and Rookeries of London, Past and Present.'   *Zoologist*, 3rd series, vol. ii. pp. 193–199. London, 1878.

NEWTON (ALFRED) : ' Rooks and Rookeries of London.'   *Zoologist*, vol. ii. pp. 441–444.   London, 1878.

HAMILTON (EDWARD) : ' The Birds of London, Past and Present, Residents and Casuals.'   *Zoologist*, vol. iii. pp. 273–291.   London, 1879.

PIGOTT (J. DIGBY) : *London Birds and London Insects.*   8vo. London, 1884.

HARTING (J. E.) : ' Bird Life in Kensington Gardens.'   *Field*, January 14, 1888.

HARTING (J. E.) : ' The Birds of Hampstead Hill,' in J. L. Lobley's *Hampstead Hill.*   4to.   London, 1889.

HAMILTON (EDWARD) : ' The Wild Birds of London.'   *Murray's Magazine.*   London, May 1889.

MILLER (CHRISTY) : *Birds of Essex.*   8vo.   London, 1890.

TRISTRAM-VALENTINE (J. T.) : *London Birds and Beasts.*   With a Preface by F. E. Beddard.   8vo.   London, 1895.

' The Birds of London.'   *Edinburgh Review.*   London, January 1898.

INDEX

PRINTED BY
SPOTTISWOODE AND CO., NEW-STREET SQUARE
LONDON